GROWING
SLOW

Also by Jennifer Dukes Lee

Stuff I'd Only Tell God

Growing Slow Bible Study

It's All Under Control

The Happiness Dare

Love Idol

My word (phrase) of the year for 2020 was "grow slow." I can't tell you how much I wish I'd had this book to lead me into those risky, restful, and fruitful days. But living a whole year under that banner convinced me that slow growth is where it's at. It's where striving makes way for joy, where change takes root, and abundance blossoms in front of our eyes. Jennifer Dukes Lee is a great leader and a kind guide, and this is a journey and a book I cannot suggest enough.

Jess Connolly, author of *You Are the Girl for the
Job* and *Breaking Free from Body Shame*

Sometimes our most important work is not what we do but what we finally learn to undo. With kindness and honesty, Jennifer Dukes Lee unfolds for us the spiritual discipline of un-hurrying our lives, from the way we spend our time to the way we define success. In a culture obsessed with power, productivity, and upward mobility, *Growing Slow* is the reminder we need to keep company with the way of Jesus.

Emily P. Freeman, *Wall Street Journal* bestselling
author of *The Next Right Thing*

Jennifer Dukes Lee always provides a breath of fresh air to the woman who needs to slow down or the woman who is discouraged because life has slowed her down. With a unique grace and time-tested wisdom, Jennifer escorts readers through the uncomfortable and often undesired journey of growing slow—because this is a journey she knows is foundational to consistently living out a beautiful life through every season.

Chrystal Evans Hurst, bestselling author and speaker

This is Jennifer's best book yet. As I worked my way through these pages, I noticed my breathing slowed, my muscles relaxed, and I sensed the invitation to look around and note all that's right in my world. We've bought the lie that God insists on and is somehow impressed by a flurry of activity and productivity, and it's cost us our very lives.

Jesus was never in a hurry. He moved at the pace of grace. Jennifer has given us a treasured inside look at her life and journey so that we might learn to treasure our own plot of land and steward it well. There aren't enough hours in the day to do it all because we were never meant to do it all. There are enough hours in the day to live in the rhythms of grace God offers us. Every tired, hurried soul needs this book. I wholeheartedly recommend it!

Susie Larson, talk radio host, national speaker, and author of
Fully Alive: Learning to Flourish—Mind, Body & Spirit

Growing Slow is a timely word for a tired and worn-out generation. In an age where the mindset of hustle and hurry leads us to burnout and exhaustion, Jennifer Dukes Lee invites us to the Ancient Way of Jesus—of growing slowly by his grace. Every woman needs to read this book!

Gretchen Saffles, author of *The Well-Watered Woman: Rooted in Truth, Growing in Grace, Flourishing in Faith* and founder of Well-Watered Women

All the hustle and hurry never gets us one step closer to the things we value most: love, connection, and meaning. From the opening chapters of *Growing Slow*, Jennifer Dukes Lee invites us to slow down and embrace everything we've worn ourselves ragged chasing after. From beginning to end, *Growing Slow* is one big, sweeping aha moment!

Wendy Speake, author of *The 40-Day Sugar Fast*

If you're tired of hearing "go big or go home," if you're looking to leave your rushed life behind and find purpose, I encourage you to pick up this book. Jennifer Dukes Lee shows you how to exchange the bigger, faster, and harder pressure for deep, lasting, purposeful living. Unhurry your heart. Rest. Grow slow.

Paula Faris, journalist, podcaster, author

Jennifer's work lifts the weight of a busy world from readers' shoulders. She pauses the rush to be more and do better, inviting us to God's way of quiet growth. Each chapter is a new kind of refreshing. This book not only teaches peace, its very pages are peaceful.

Phylicia Masonheimer, founder & CEO of Every Woman a Theologian

Jennifer Dukes Lee is a careful wordsmith in a world full of sound-bites. The message of simplicity in *Growing Slow* is one I personally crave—the right one to help the exhausted reader find freedom.

Lisa Whittle, author, Bible teacher, podcast host

Growing Slow is an invitation every hurried soul needs. If you're overwhelmed, anxious, or weary, then pause and walk with Jennifer through these pages. Your heart will be freer, your mind calmer, and your load lighter by the time you're finished.

Holley Gerth, life coach and bestselling author
of *The Powerful Purpose of Introverts*

Some books are good; others are needed. This one is both. A life well-lived for the gospel is not measured in accomplishments and results, but in how well we love God and love others, so we must trade the world's quick and easy mindset for a slow but steady heart. *Growing Slow* feels like a coffee date with a seasoned and trusted friend. Turn off your notifications and savor the conversation with Jennifer inside.

Michelle Myers and Somer Phoebus, lead
communicators of She Works HIS Way

Every time I picked up *Growing Slow*, it didn't take long for the tears to start falling as I felt a weight lift from my shoulders with Jennifer's words. She speaks truth, reminding us that growing slow means growing deep roots. This book is a needed message for all of us as we fight the urge to hurry through life.

Caitlin Henderson, author of *Faith, Farming, and Family*

In a world bent on "more and quickly," *Growing Slow* takes the farm road less traveled and eloquently maps a path to fulfillment by embracing the slow and holy, here and now. Jennifer Dukes Lee's words are the nourishment our hurried hearts need in order to pause, praise, prepare, and pace for optimal soul growth.

Meredith Bernard, ThisFarmWife.com

JENNIFER
DUKES LEE

GROWING
SLOW

>>>>>>————<<<<<<

LESSONS ON UN-HURRYING
YOUR HEART FROM AN
ACCIDENTAL FARM GIRL

ZONDERVAN
BOOKS

ZONDERVAN BOOKS

Growing Slow
Copyright © 2021, 2024 by Jennifer Dukes Lee

Published in Grand Rapids, Michigan, by Zondervan. Zondervan is a registered trademark of The Zondervan Corporation, L.L.C., a wholly owned subsidiary of HarperCollins Christian Publishing, Inc.

Requests for information should be addressed to customercare@harpercollins.com.

Zondervan titles may be purchased in bulk for educational, business, fundraising, or sales promotional use. For information, please email SpecialMarkets@Zondervan.com.

ISBN 978-0-310-36946-2 (softcover)
ISBN 978-0-310-36045-2 (audio)

Library of Congress Cataloging-in-Publication Data

Names: Lee, Jennifer Dukes, author.
Title: Growing slow : lessons on un-hurrying your heart from an accidental farm girl / Jennifer Dukes Lee.
Description: Grand Rapids : Zondervan, 2021. | Includes bibliographical references. | Summary: "Growing Slow is a timely, inspiring, and insightful read in which author and farm wife Jennifer Dukes Lee shows the way to unhurrying our hearts, embracing the relaxed rhythms of nature, and discovering the meaningful gift of slow growth"—Provided by publisher.
Identifiers: LCCN 2020045495 (print) | LCCN 2020045496 (ebook) | ISBN 9780310360438 (hardcover) | ISBN 9780310360445 (ebook)
Subjects: LCSH: Peace of mind—Religious aspects—Christianity. | Stress management for women. | Rhythm—Religious aspects—Christianity.
Classification: LCC BV4908.5 .L44 2021 (print) | LCC BV4908.5 (ebook) | DDC 248.8/43—dc23
LC record available at https://lccn.loc.gov/2020045495
LC ebook record available at https://lccn.loc.gov/2020045496

The author is represented by Alive Literary Agency, www.aliveliterary.com.

Cover design: Micah Kandros
Cover illustration: Anastasiia Gevko / Shutterstock
Interior design: Denise Froehlich

$PrintCode

To the generations before us,
who have cared for the land on which we stand,
and to future generations who will inherit
the responsibility to love her well.

CONTENTS

PART 4: WINTER REST

A NOTE TO THE READER

To the beautiful soul holding this book,
        I find it so remarkable that God didn't bring us to earth as fully matured, fully grown, fully functioning human beings. Rather, we showed up on the planet as babies, needing to learn and grow and love and walk over time. We are all *becoming*—one thought at a time, one mistake at a time, one success at a time, one choice at a time, one relationship at a time, one breath at a time, one season at a time. It takes a lifetime to become and become and become again.

We are, by virtue of our created existence, born to grow slowly, over time, into the people God wants us to be. And that's where the beauty happens: in the becoming.

The same is true for books. While a book isn't a living, breathing creature, it can feel that way, as its message widens and matures past an author's vision, expanding into more of what God intended it to be. I know this to be true, because I've watched it happen with the book you're holding in your hands.

From the beginning, *Growing Slow* was the story of my heart, told from the voice of a farmer's wife who, like Jesus, is especially fond of farming metaphors. This book was a tiny, word-wrapped seed that sprouted, then bloomed, then spread like a vine, wrapping around hearts across the globe. I wrote this book over the course of a year—from the spring of 2019 to the spring of 2020—and since then, I have observed with surprise how this message has become a richer, fuller version of what I originally envisioned.

To be sure, *Growing Slow* is still, and will always be, a message that challenges you to slow your life down and spend each day on the things that matter most. It is still, and will always be, a gentle call away from a life of hustle and an invitation to truly enjoy your life.

But, because of the rambunctious, remarkable beauty of becoming, this book became something more—not only for me, but for the thousands of people who took the message to heart. As it turns out, *Growing Slow* became more than a message about slowing down. It also became a timely summons to embrace the season you're living in right now, whatever season that may be, in the same way we embrace the seasons on our farm as part of a healthy ecosystem.

On this farm, one of the things I've learned about the land is that every season has a reason—spring, summer, autumn, and winter. No season skips a turn, even the seasons that carry discomfort and suffering. Furthermore, the most pleasant seasons of all, the ones with wagons mounded with grain and skies lit up with fireflies, don't last forever.

The same is true for us. We pass through seasons, slowly.

In spring, like a farmer, we plant seeds into relationships, ministries, and businesses. In this season of perennial hope, God also plants seeds into the soil of our hearts, tending us like the Divine Farmer he is.

Then, in summer, we stand back and take joy in seeing how God is growing something beautiful from the seeds we planted in faith long ago. If you've watched a human grow from childhood into adulthood, or if you've reached a milestone in your career, you understand well the joy of a summer season.

In autumn, we celebrate the incredible fruit that has grown in our lives. Yet we also find ourselves feeling wistful. We may even feel the need to mourn, because the things we worked so hard for, the things we always saw on the horizon, the reasons we went out into our fields in the first place . . . *are over*.

And then comes winter. On our farm, that means the days grow shorter, the nights grow darker, and a cold discomfort weighs heavy in the air. Winter seasons happen inside of us as well, when our very souls shiver inside the iceboxes of disappointment and despair. We would prefer to live in the warmth and light of spring and summer, or the fruitful season of autumn harvest. But lo, we find ourselves in the bleak midwinter, when frosty wind moans and water is like a stone.[1]

It can be easy to think that you can neatly fit seasons into boxes marked as "good" or "bad." But that's not true. Each season can bring suffering, and each season can bring inexplicable joy. Just as a drought or windstorm can wreak havoc on a summer field of corn, an out-of-the-blue storm can level you in the summer of your life. And winter offers more than the heaviness of discouragement and darkness. Winter can bring you unexpected joy as you find Jesus cupping your pain in his own nail-scarred hands.

Each season is part of the beauty of your own becoming. Each is a mix of the hard and the good. And perhaps this is so we might learn to trust God in the hard and praise him in the good.

We are not meant to rush from one season to the next, chasing after a paradisaical existence that doesn't exist this side of heaven. Rather, we grow most deeply when we dwell fully within each season, finding Jesus walking throughout the fields of our hearts, tending us with love each step of the way.

It's in that spirit that I celebrate the re-release of *Growing Slow*, now in paperback.

Whether you've read the book before or this is your first time with these words, I invite you to read *Growing Slow* through the lens of dwelling within each season, avoiding the temptation to rush through them, even in times of uncertainty. I also invite you to read this book as it was intended to be read: slowly. It is split into four sections—spring, summer, autumn, and winter. You might consider starting in the section that best represents the current season of nature where you live, as many have done. Or you can start in the soul-season you find yourself in right now. For further reflection, consider the *Growing Slow Bible Study: A 6-Week Guided Journey to Un-Hurrying Your Heart* and its accompanying videos, which were filmed on our farm across the four seasons and are available to you for free. To access the free videos, visit www.GrowingSlowBook .com/Resources. When prompted, enter your email address and the code for access: JDLGrowingSlow.

As you read, may you see Jesus in each season where you dwell. May you find the language to praise him in the good, and the courage to trust him in the hard. And may you see each season as a part of the beautiful process of God growing you, as you become fully who he longs for you to be.

With love,

Jennifer

READY, SET, SLOW: AN INTRODUCTION

Some stories arrive in this world because their authors scribbled them onto a running list of ideas they keep hidden in a desk drawer. Other stories—maybe the best ones of all—simply insist to be written. This story, *Growing Slow*, is one of these.

It's a story about why we are all in a hurry yet afraid to slow the pace. It's a story about our desire for a simpler life—and our persistent refusal to take hold of it. It's a story about the nagging sense of dissatisfaction with what we're growing in our lives. We wonder if we're really doing enough with these numbered days we've been given.

Ultimately, it's a story about why we are all in the chase in the first place. It boils down to this: we want love, connection, fruitful lives, and meaningful growth.

We tend to believe that to get what we want, we have to pick up the pace. But as it turns out, the truth is counterintuitive. We have to be willing to do something dramatic—radical, even. It will go against the grain of everything we've been taught.

We have to be willing to slow the pace. The good life we're after cannot be secured by running hard, *but by growing slow.*

This awareness shifted something in me in the middle of a very hard year on our fifth-generation family farm in a quiet corner of Iowa. Unrelenting rains kept us out of the fields at harvest, and then the rain returned to torment us when we tried to plant those same fields in the spring. Clouds stacked up on one another like gigantic, thundering anvils. Every morning, I would stand at the kitchen window, overlooking the "back 80"—the 80 acres that roll out like a black carpet from the backyard. Raindrops struck the house with such force, it sounded as if we lived in a tin can. I could barely see through a shower of a trillion watery bullets, whizzing with dead aim on our fields.

Our hearts and hopes and hands were calloused. We needed reassurance that good things would grow once more in these fields. Hard as it was, we knew we needed to wait on God, the very same God who has stood sovereign over this land since he first spoke it into being.

At supper, our family of four would bow our heads over plates of steaming pork roast and root vegetables. We prayed for our land and for the rains to stop. We scribbled furiously in our prayer journals. At our little country church with the white steeple pointing to heaven, our church family held hands across the aisles and sealed our eyes shut tight while we prayed for all the farmers who were at the ends of their ropes, calling into the farm crisis hotlines. Our souls begged the Lord to grant us peace in the midst of the panic.

Deep down, we truly did believe that the Lord would come through—maybe not in our timing, nor with the yields we would want. It would be a growing-slow kind of year—slow into the fields, slow out of them—but these fields *would* be planted. We rehearsed God's ancient promises and his pattern of provision in the created world. We reminded ourselves what Jesus said about how plants grow, which is simply this: "They do not labor or spin."[1] Sure enough, in all my years as a farmer's wife, I've never once seen a corn plant freaking out.

We needed to find the courage to be still, to give everything a little bit of time, to let it all grow slow.

In the middle of that hard year, it dawned on me: what I

believed to be true for the *land*, I didn't completely believe for me, in my grow-fast life.

What if, in a growing-slow year, I deliberately embraced a Growing Slow life? What if I set aside all I'd been taught about achievement and ambition and goals? What if I stopped treating all of life like an emergency? It seemed audacious.

What would I stand to gain? And what would I stand to lose?

Because the truth of the matter was, I had always been in a hurry. And honestly? That had worked out pretty well if you looked at my resume.

I set out on my life's journey with bright-eyed enthusiasm and energy, with the hopes of building a wonderful life. And I do have a life that I love, with a husband I love, two beautiful daughters whom I love, and work that I love as an author and book editor. We live on land that has been loved well by five generations of my husband's family, along with the wives before me who stood at their kitchen windows overlooking the Lee land: Joyce, Eunice, Emma, Maria. I thank the Lord that I found faith after nearly giving in to an ambiguous, nagging agnosticism in my twenties. And despite the million ways that I ran after wrong things, I hope I'm making a positive mark on the world with integrity, kindness, and generosity.

But my body, this scaffolding that carries me along life's journey, began to destabilize. I became fearful that my ready-set-go pace would kill me—maybe not physically, but emotionally, mentally, and, perhaps, spiritually. I have always cared a little too much about productivity, but I could tell that my warp-speed pace meant that I was doing C-minus work on the things I cared about most. I simply couldn't carry it all as I ran around like a crazy person trying to make some kind of difference in the world. Worst of all, I knew that I wasn't fully present for the best moments unfolding around me. I wasn't sure I even liked the person I had become.

That Growing Slow year on the farm gave me time and space

to ponder life's meaning. Here's what I learned: in the scramble to grow a purposeful life, we accidentally forfeit too much—a settledness with what we already have, a sense of peace with what already is, and a connectedness with the people right here with us.

You can get so rushed chasing a certain kind of remarkable life that you miss the fact that you're already standing inside the one God gave you.

The Diagnosis

I've always been a high-capacity person who can handle a lot at once. Until I couldn't. My body was betraying me. (Or maybe I was betraying my body by pushing it so hard.) I was well into my forties, and had the ambition of my twenty-three-year-old self, but something was off. I was tired, had an aching gut, was sleeping horribly, and felt on edge and jittery.

I wondered if something more sinister was having its way with my body, some strange disease.

And then there was unexplained memory loss. I forgot to show up for lunch with a friend, forgot to feed the barn cats, forgot to pay a bill, forgot to pick up my daughter from school for a dentist appointment. Small lapses, perhaps, but obligations I never would have missed before. I couldn't find the right words for simple objects—I told my husband I had put the pots and pans in the washing machine; I had meant to say, "the bedsheets." I honestly wondered if it was early onset dementia, which sounds so dramatic, but the forgetfulness shook me.

Emotionally, I didn't recognize myself. I laughed less and cried more, but not at the sappy romantic comedy. Tears sprung mostly when I got angry, irritated, or overwhelmed.

One afternoon, I found myself in the office of a functional medicine doctor. He's the type of doctor who thoroughly audits your whole self—body, mind, spirit, soul—rather than merely scribbling off a prescription and sending you to the pharmacy to fix whatever is broken.

I ended up in his office as a last resort after many appointments during which several vials of blood were given, urine cups peed in, heartbeats monitored, organs scanned. No tests showed anything wrong.

Could this doctor just tell me what was wrong, give it a name, and fix it so I could be all that the world needed me to be? And could he do it *fast*?

Sitting in the chair next to his desk, I tilted my chin toward the ceiling, counted tiles, and hoped my posture could somehow keep my tears locked in. Being emotionally naked and raw like that made me uncomfortable.

But tears ran down my cheeks and under my collar, leaving me hot and blotchy.

"Jennifer," the doctor said, "this is a severe case of stress. All the signs are there: low energy, insomnia, anxiety, overwhelm, an overloaded mind."

Friend, let me be honest with you: this didn't make sense to me. I knew hurried, stressed-out people. I wasn't one of them. Was I?

At the time, I was sure I wasn't. I thrive on deadlines. Hard work doesn't intimidate me; in fact, it invigorates me. Besides, I had built margin into my life, heavily pruning my schedule years before that moment with the doctor. Furthermore, I had been teaching and writing for several years on finding peace, even in the midst of a busy life.

I told him all that, and he listened. Then he paused, crossed his arms over his chest, and said, "I believe you. But this isn't about your schedule or calendar. This is about your heart and your soul."

There was no pill to fix this. No surgery. No trip to the pharmacy.

The "cure" would have to be an inside job. Something needed

to change. I needed to let go of the belief that I was behind or that
I should have been further along by then.

I had a hurried heart. And I had to do something to un-hurry it.

I needed to learn how to grow slow.

An Invitation

That's where you find me now—on a life-changing journey to un-
hurry my heart and entrust my endeavors to Jesus.

This book is my messy account of moving from a place of
depleting hurry to a place of sustaining trust and rest.

I need to be frank with you. I didn't write this book because I
knew everything. I wrote it because I needed to relearn everything
all over again, like a kindergartener being told by her teacher to stop
running in the hallways.

I wrote this book because I didn't want to get to the end of my
life, look back, and regret who I'd become. That I'd mistaken success for meaning. That life was a blur. That I ran so hard, I forgot
how to walk with God.

I wrote this book because I got tired of living as if I'm afraid of
being late to my own funeral.[2]

In the midst of this wild experiment of embracing slowness,
Jesus has been smashing my long-cherished ideas of "growth" into
a million pieces. The world rewards fast growth over slow growth.
It rewards overnight sensations, the first, the best, and the fastest.
And who doesn't like rewards?

But there is a richer reward waiting for us when we embrace
slowness and stop idolizing speed. A Growing Slow life gives you
what your heart really longs for: permission to take a beat and to
take a breath; grace to try again; courage to walk instead of run; and
space to live in the astonishing and wild love of Christ.

Will you come with me? I suspect that you need to un-hurry

your heart, too. You need the courage to slow down. You want to stop being afraid of what you'll miss when you make the choice to grow slow.

Come with me, friend. Come to my farm, and stand barefooted with me at the edge of our fields, under this expansive sky. Cup the soil in your hands, and let it fall through your fingers, slowly. Stay here a while, and tip your face toward heaven. Above us, the geese will V north, across the striking blue, cloudless sky of the day. Pheasants—thick-throated in their crowing—will dart through the evergreens. Let's stay here, long enough for day's last light to fade to charcoal. Overhead, Orion's belt will slide across the sky.

Let's consider the things we are growing and ponder the depth of their roots. Let's ease our way back toward an un-hurried life where seasons are embraced as sacred and holy. Let's call out the value in the small, good things we are growing. These are things that matter deeply.

Now, let's talk.

Let's really talk about why we aren't slowing it down, even though we know we should.

Let's talk about how we've heard this invitation before—to stop hurrying—but we ignore it. Our hearts are still hurried. Why?

Let's talk.

The truth that we are fully known and fully loved by God beckons us. So let's talk about how we try to make it more than that. How we distort God's love, making it about earning and consuming and growing a bunch of stuff that looks and feels like God's love.

The better halves of our hearts push against the temptation to constantly keep everything moving forward. Deep down, we long for little more than living like we really believe that what God says about us is true.

That small things matter.

That the tiny seeds we are planting will grow into something meaningful.

That we haven't disappointed God.

I'll bet you a side of bacon and a wagonload of harvested corn that you want the same things I do. You want to stop running around in search of love and meaning. You want something better than burnout.

This doesn't mean you'll stop growing good things. On the contrary. You will get your hands dirty in these fields.

Together, we will press seeds deep down, knowing that new life starts in dark, unseen places. That's where the story gets good——in the moment before the miracle ruptures the earth. That's the moment of breakthrough. Oh, it might take time for that breakthrough. There are moments when you will stand before your field of dreams, with calloused hands shoved into pockets, while not a single shoot bursts forth with life.

Despite your best efforts.

Despite your earnest prayers.

Despite the exasperating impression that every other field around yours is abloom, alive.

And yours? It looks . . . dead.

It's time to embrace a different story about everything you're growing. It's time to have faith to believe what your eyes cannot see. The most beautiful things in this grand old world began as seeds that waited in the dark.

Every oak was first a buried acorn.

Every corn plant on our farm was first a dormant, hard-coated seed, waiting for permission to crack open—a tedious and glorious breaking—before pushing against the earth with striking force, then creeping skyward one steady micron at a time.

Your seeds aren't dead. They are waiting. The darkness under the soil isn't a graveyard. Your seeds are very much alive, gaining the strength necessary to push into the light—and thrive.

Together we will grow things slowly, and together, we ourselves will grow slow.

How to Use This Book to Un-Hurry Your Heart

Every scratched-out word of this story is how God un-hurried the heart of this accidental farm girl. My prayer is that he will use each one of those words to un-hurry *yours* as well.

This book is not about giving you a bunch of new things to do. Instead, it's a book that will ask you to adopt a new mindset—a Growing Slow mindset.

In order to live with a Growing Slow mindset, you will let go of the popular idea that purposeful living is synonymous with hurry.

I suspect that some of you are thinking, *I know I should slow down, but I also believe I should have achieved more by now so I've got to hustle to make up for lost opportunities.* Maybe you believe you've let God down by not making a bigger impact.

If you're looking for a book that helps you dream bigger dreams, this is not the book for you. This isn't a book that will move you upward, but one that will move you inward, to the heart of things.

Growing Slow is not a girl-boss message to motivate you to take charge or do more. There's a place for those books, and because of the way I'm wired, I could have totally written a real kick-in-the-pants book called *Growing Fast*—complete with actionable steps and motivational tips to help you do a bunch more stuff.

But this is not that book, and that is not the way I want to live my life anymore. Maybe we all need permission to dial it back, instead of instruction on how to rev it all up.

This world is in such a rush that psychologists now say people suffer from "hurry sickness," defined as the "constant need to do more, faster, even when there's no objective reason to be in such a rush."[3]

We need a way to recover from hurry sickness. Healing will come from the inside out, in our hearts, where Jesus dwells and where the wild things grow. This Jesus actually sees us as we grow good things in our families, friendships, and faith journeys.

Growing Slow is a collection of personal stories and biblical insights I've gleaned during my life on the farm. But this book is much more than my story. It will become yours, as you walk hand in hand with God through your own fields and gardens. At the end of each chapter, you will have space to personally remember, reflect, and return to the land.

I wrote this book over the course of a year, through an entire 365-day growing season. Every word was written with the land outside my kitchen window in view. Through the window, I was a quiet witness to each changing season: spring planting, summer growth, autumn harvest, and winter rest, as we await another year of slow and meaningful growth.

It was a beautiful year, and it was a hard year. Maybe a bit like yours?

Together, we'll learn lessons as the earth is turned, then planted, then greened up and up and up, until the rows touch and roots deepen. One cool morning, we'll look out the window and see the first signs of a gentle yellowing, and then, days later, a crisping of every leaf. Some afternoon, we'll watch as farmers reenter the fields and, like barbers, slowly clip it away until nothing is left but empty, quiet fields, soon to be buried in snow. All good things come to a close, a necessary ending: winter.

It's been right here all along—the land teaching us how to unhurry our hurry-sick hearts. Land speaks stunning truths through Scripture.

The Hebrew word for land is *eretz*. It is the fifth most frequently used noun in the Hebrew Bible, after the Hebrew words for LORD, son, God, and king.[4] The land is more than a backdrop for the stories told in the Bible. Rather, the land is a leading character in the magnificent biblical narrative, from the very beginning when God made life in a garden.

The lessons Jesus drew from the land were clear to first-century agrarian culture, and we don't want to miss them in this modern age—the vineyards, wheat, threshing floors, gleaning, fields for grazing. Rain signaled God's provision. Literal droughts tested the faith of the people. Jesus was known not only as the true vine, but the good shepherd, who minds both the land and its creatures.

The land, with its seasons and complexity, is central to God's promise to his people, not only to the nomadic Israelites in search of a place to call home, but to each one of us, in our everyday lives at Target, Starbucks, the chemo infusion center, the nursing home, the altar, and the laundry room.

When I began to write this book, a verse guided me at every turn:

To everything there is a season, a time for every purpose under heaven.[5]

A complex set of verses follows that opening line in Ecclesiastes 3, revealing that all of life is a seasonal paradox—a time to be born, a time to die, a time to plant, a time to uproot, a time to dance, and even a time to mourn.

In a world obsessed with "instant," these verses reveal that there is a time for everything, and everything in its time.

That's the simple, complicated truth about life and the land—marked alternately by healing and death and joy and pain and sorrow and celebration. We are tempted to live only in the good of Ecclesiastes 3. We want the joy and the dancing. We are desperate for comfort, growth, and progress.

However, there are times for *all* things, even the devastating things and the slow, boring things. Let's take our time and explore the complexity of each season, wrestling if we must. For it's here in the dirt of these fields that God teaches us about ourselves and, more importantly, about himself.

Long ago, at the beginning of time, God created the first human, and he did it in an incredibly intimate way.

He started with soil.

He knelt down, cupped dirt in his hands, breathed life into it.

God gave this first human a name: Adam. In Hebrew, Adam is *adamah*. It's a word that means land, ground, or soil. Our story began with a fistful of soil and the breath of God.

That's how this story begins as well. With you. With me. With soil.

With God.

Let's go nice and easy.

Ready, set, slow.

REMEMBER

The tiny seeds I am planting into
dark, unseen places will grow
into something meaningful.

REFLECT

As we begin, take a few moments to reflect on the things
you are growing. List them here.

....

....

....

....

....

In what ways do you feel pressure to do more, be more in
a "grow fast" culture?

....

....

....

Do you think it's practically possible to "grow slow" with
the demands upon you?

....

....

....

What do you most hope to gain from this journey?

....

....

....

RETURN

At the end of each chapter, we will return
to the soil, where our stories began in
the very first farm on earth—the Garden
of Eden. Here, we will recall how God
cupped humanity in his hands and
breathed life into us all. God cups *you* in
his hands. He breathes new life into you.

What area of your life do you most need God to breathe
new life into today? Tell him about it now, in the space
provided.

....

....

....

....

....

....

....

....

....

....

PART 1

SPRING PLANTING

For behold, the winter is past; the rain is over
and gone. The flowers appear on the earth,
the time of singing has come, and the voice
of the turtledove is heard in our land.

SONG OF SOLOMON 2:11–12 ESV

CHAPTER 1

PERMISSION TO BE UN-SPECTACULAR

I am an accidental farm girl. I never intended to live in a place where pigs outnumber people by a significant margin, stray cows trample your rosebushes, and the school hosts a "Drive Your Tractor to School Day" every spring. In fact, my intention as a child growing up in Iowa was to escape it!

I was raised in a small town, nestled down by the North Raccoon River. It was a blink-and-you'll-miss-it kind of town. The closest McDonald's or JCPenney was a half hour away. I wanted skyscrapers, streetlights, subways, and swarms of people on humming sidewalks. When I was eighteen, those dreams seemed within reach—with enough hustle, of course. My acceptance to university felt like a ticket to freedom.

It was the first day of college orientation at Iowa State University in Ames. Hundreds of us sat in fold-down auditorium chairs with padded seats while a motivational speaker paced in front of us, her high heels clicking with each step. "What do you want to be famous for?" she asked.

Her question hung in the air. She paused long enough for us

to fantasize about our answers. Visions of who we would be at age twenty-five, thirty-five, forty-five materialized. Although fame had never been a goal I'd articulated, the question awakened something in me, perhaps in all of us.

She had just delivered a sparkling invitation to be spectacular.

For a girl who grew up in obscurity—with a cornfield in her backyard and silos in her skyline—the idea was incredibly appealing. Who doesn't long to be known?

In that moment, I began to dream about my future self as an award-winning journalist, perhaps on Capitol Hill. The daydream offered the promise of a Pulitzer, and I believed in its possibility. I would make a mark on the world. People wearing neckties would answer my calls and care about my opinion. Of course, my life would also be characterized by charity and decency. Some future husband and I would create extraordinarily bright and well-behaved children who would eat all their vegetables. And if I got my spiritual act together, I would finally take hold of the faith that my Sunday School teachers had tried to instill in me.

And then, in the years stacked on top of years, I ran fast and furious toward the making of a spectacular life.

Back in the college auditorium, my barely-adult self didn't really want fame. I simply wanted a life of meaning—a noble aim planted within each of us by God himself.

We all crave a meaningful life. This is good and holy. But in the quest for meaning, we get mixed up, turned around, and accidentally end up constantly in a hurry. We rush to grow successful businesses, a more potent faith, robust bank accounts, and, if we are parents, spiritually-grounded children. We climb proverbial mountains and dream bigger dreams. Any obstacles can be obliterated swiftly by the right amount of self-help dynamite.

That sort of existence may, indeed, lead us somewhere

spectacular. But the costs are high: we end up feeling rushed, often anxious and out of sorts, fearful that we are falling behind.

Here, the hurried heart is born and then nurtured in a million ways by a culture that idolizes bigger, harder, faster. This was the life I accidentally chose—a life of running hard, scaling fast, and chasing results.

Do you know the bruising, try-hard way of the hurried heart?

A hurried heart manifests itself in both big and little ways—from the way you feel about your life's worth to the way you respond to being stuck in a long line at Starbucks. It's the way you react when you hop on Instagram, see everybody winning, and conclude that your contributions seem meaningless.

Take a moment to reflect on your life and consider whether you show signs of a hurried heart:

> You feel like you are working harder than ever but can never get ahead.
> Periods of slowness make you feel uneasy, like you should be doing something productive.
> You check your phone immediately upon waking up.
> You get frustrated in traffic or in long lines at grocery stores.
> You rarely make time for play.
> You feel a sense of urgency to get things done; sometimes this keeps you up at night.
> You can't remember the last time you felt bored.
> You think if a person is bored, she might be a little lazy.
> You pride yourself on your ability to multitask.
> You never feel you've done enough.
> Delays or unexpected obstacles upset or irritate you.
> You've asked yourself questions like, "Does anything I do even matter?" or "What do I have to show for my life?"

Not all of these will resonate, but even if a few do, you probably have a hurried heart. Let's be honest: almost all of us do, but we don't know how to tap the brakes.

We want to believe a slower life is possible but fear we will miss out if we don't keep the pace. So we bend to the pressure to go big and get public, and that's exactly the moment when we miss the gift of slowness, even the gift of obscurity. We chase after something that keeps slipping through our fingers. This grasp at an elusive state of spectacular-ness never ends, for it always seems just out of reach. Which means everybody keeps moving a little faster to touch a moving target.

Adult Jennifer understands what College Jennifer didn't yet know in that auditorium. We don't need permission to be spectacular.

We need permission to be *un-spectacular.*

We need permission to stop trying to build something bigger, to have the right conversations with the right people. To stop sucking in our guts, to stop waiting for the kids' nap time so we can finally get to our important work. We need permission to stop idolizing brawn and might. We need permission to take our time, to marvel, to wonder and ponder and savor, and to move at the un-hurried pace of Christ. Time is not a commodity to be used but a gem to be treasured.

We need permission to grow slow.

Just a Small-Town Girl

Perhaps ironically, I grew up at the speed of slow in that tiny town near the trickling North Raccoon River. They say life is a marathon, not a sprint, and somehow the stars aligned so I could begin my life story in Marathon, Iowa. All the streets were named after Greek places like Attica and Sparta. And one cold February day, my parents brought me home from the hospital to our century-old house on Athens Street. That house was my home until I left for college.

Life as a small-town girl felt exceptionally un-spectacular. The three words I uttered almost every day were, "Mom, I'm bored." Yet amidst the boredom, there was a stability that I didn't appreciate until later in life.

The people who held me at church as a baby bought my Girl Scout cookies and cheered me and my siblings on at basketball games. They attended our baptisms and our weddings. Later, we attended their fiftieth wedding anniversaries and their funerals.

Life was a series of church basement potlucks, long visits from the Avon lady, bike rides to the gravel pit, popping tar bubbles on the road with our bare toes, May Day baskets, and tree climbing. There were parades, Fourth of July picnics, ice cream socials, and Saturday night gatherings called the "Good Ol' Days." Every activity—a pancake feed at the American Legion hall, a community potluck at the park—was advertised by writing the Who, What, and Where in permanent marker on poster boards, duct-taping those boards to a barrel, and setting that barrel right out in the middle of Main Street.

No one was a stranger in Marathon. I knew everyone at the bank, the grain elevator, the hardware store. Local characters had nicknames like Spot, Brick, Tuck, Buck, and Mountain Man. Mom would get mail addressed simply to, "Mama D., Marathon, Iowa, 50565" because the postman knew the slot in which to slip the letter. When Mom was hospitalized with cancer, our hometown responded in ways that speak to the meaning and connection our small, slow life afforded us. In those two weeks, Mama D. received more than 500 cards and letters. People made the three-hour trip to sit with her while she recovered in the hospital. When she got home, Marathon women had left casseroles for her in the refrigerator.

We always left the door unlocked.

Looking back, I am overcome with nostalgic affection for those days. In this culture of speed, I grieve what's been lost.

I am certain my childhood sounds like a scene ripped from the Hallmark Channel—quaint, charming, peaceful.

Let's look closer. Over the years, the ethic of bigger/better/faster began to disintegrate the fabric of our little town. In the 1980s farm crisis, several of my schoolmates' parents lost their farms and were forced to move off their land. Bankruptcies and suicides shattered farmsteads and communities across America. One afternoon, I watched as four vacant buildings in our town were simultaneously demolished with dynamite. Those doomed storefronts had once held life. Inside those buildings, I sat for my first haircut and ordered my first chocolate malt. But the stores were shuttered when their owners could no longer compete with the bigger and "better" offerings in larger nearby towns, and so, to "clean up" the town, crews blew those buildings to smithereens.

Big and fast trampled over small and slow, leaving a footprint the approximate size of Walmart.

When I left that small, slow life in Marathon, I had no desire to return.

Years later, I wrote an essay for the *Des Moines Register* declaring that I'd never live in rural America again due to its decline and lack of career options.

To that, God seemed to say, "Ha!"

The life I declared all but dead is now the one I'm living, a mere hundred miles from the tiny town I first called home.

Sociologists call people like my husband and me "U-turn farmers," a term used to describe people who have been tugged away from the city to return to their rural roots.

In many ways, life in my current town is similar to the one I knew as a child. Everyone knows everyone, not only by their last names but by their pickup trucks. I know my bank teller, not by the nameplate at her station but by her face in the gymnasium bleachers. I know our neighbors, not because they wave to me on the highway but because we show up for each other at baby showers and funerals and in the back pew with tears streaming. We don't have Good Ol' Days celebrations like we had in Marathon, but I do see my childhood community echoing forward to find me here—in another town, in another decade. Our little town here in Lyon County is famous for its annual Fourth of July celebration, complete with a pancake breakfast, a parade, a demolition derby, and a contest where greased pigs are set loose in a ring to be captured.

One of the most beautiful parts of small-town living is the way people take care of each other, in the same way I remember people taking care of our family when Mom got cancer.

When someone gets a bad diagnosis here, someone else will invariably plan a "benefit dinner." Just like in Marathon, someone will write the Who, What, and Where on a poster board and set a barrel smack-dab in the middle of Main Street to advertise it. Farmers will haul out a gigantic grill and make pork sandwiches. Local ladies will make pounds of potato salad, piled like cumulonimbus clouds in gallon pails. Everyone will show up.

If you spent a year here with me, you'd notice right away that the rhythms are slow and natural—enforced by the seasons and kept in motion by God, the keeper of the tempo.

The rhythms are so slow that "you can hear the sun set," as Rob puts it. Rob and Michelle are dear friends who live a mile south of us, and Scott and I have spent many summer nights sitting with them under the roof of their screened-in porch, enjoying Pinot Noir poured into stemmed glasses, while the sun slips out of sight, turning the clouds into floating pink feathers. When the sun sets, the birds change their tune from bright singing to a distinctly different sound. They call each other back to the roost. Soon, night noises emerge, a chorus of crickets, frogs, and locusts.

But between the two—the day sounds and the night sounds—there is a pause, an absolute silence that feels like both a benediction and a new beginning.

This is the sound of Growing Slow.

It sounds magical, yes?

Still, so many of us—even here in the peaceful countryside—fight against natural rhythms that are so blatantly obvious you can hear them in a nightly sunset lullaby. Don't let the romanticism fool you. We still succumb to enchantments of faster, bigger, stronger every single day.

Like hurried people everywhere, we dismiss the wonder of ordinary life. Despite our desires for sustainable growth, we can't quite shake the allure of "more" and "fast."

More growth.

More influence.

More money.

More knowledge.

More followers.

More approval.

More success.

More comfort.

More progress in our marriages.

More fruit in our parenting.

Like almost everyone I know, we live on the edge of exhaustion. There's always an itch to hurry, to check our phones, to monitor progress, to wonder why we aren't further along by now.

We are tempted to structure our lives around accomplishment and quantitative results. We suffer from distraction and impatience. The concept of Growing Slow in a culture of speed sounds nice but unrealistic. Won't we get behind? Won't people think we're lazy?

But deep down in our hearts, all of us—no matter where we live—are desperate to slow down. We want to know it's possible.

Is it?

What if we could reclaim the peace and connection of a slower way? What if we could live life more thoughtfully in the places where we have been planted? Or, what if we can't? If we dial it all back, will we be trampled underfoot, like those demolished buildings in Marathon, left as rubble in the race for spectacular? Have we reached the tipping point, and it's too far gone? Is the dream of a simpler life really nothing more than nostalgia?

I am convinced that we *can* have a simpler life by making deliberate and thoughtful choices.

With a Growing Slow mindset, we will harness the rhythm of our ordinary lives, making a choice to protest the accelerated pace that always demands more. This decision will ask a lot of us. We will need to change how we work, how we measure "success," how we love, and how we live.

This is a complete revolution. A Growing Slow mindset will rescue us from the rim of exhausted living.

Come to the land, friend. Come to the fields of our farm. And come to the Holy Land of our spiritual ancestors, for it has much to teach us. I believe with all my heart that our spiritual ancestors would tell us this: *It's okay to grow slow, because when you grow slow, you grow deep.*

Early Christians from a place called Colossae would have understood the value of deep-rooted growth. The Colossians lived in a city surrounded by fields that yielded olives and figs. Farmers pastured sheep, which contributed to a thriving wool industry. In Latin, the dyed red wool was called colossinum, an indication of the city's namesake.[1]

Deep roots mattered on those farms—and in the hearts of first-century believers. In Paul's letter to the Colossians, he spoke to them in terms they would have understood: farming terms. He wrote:

> Let your roots grow down into him, and let your lives be built on him. Then, your faith will grow strong in the truth you were taught, and you will overflow with thankfulness.[2]

This slow growth, *this* is what we were made for—with roots growing deep, growing strong in truth. This is the way to sustainable growth in our families, our friendships, and our faith journeys. It is possible.

And it is the way of Christ.

The Slow Growth Movement

An entire international movement has emerged out of our innate desire for a decelerated life. In the same decade that those buildings were demolished on Marathon's main street, the Slow Movement was born on the other side of the world, in Italy.

It was 1986. Carlo Petrini protested the opening of a fast food restaurant in Piazza di Spagna, Rome, which spurred a global movement toward "slow food." Carlo better not get between me and my Taco John's Potato Olés with nacho cheese, but I do appreciate what emerged from his protest—a deeper appreciation of local food, traditional cooking, and artisan production. The idea: eating should be about quality and pleasure, not the swiftness of production.

The slow food philosophy took hold. Over the years, the concept expanded to slow education, slow fashion, slow travel, even slow sex. Whole cities have adopted the philosophy of being a slow city, or "Cittaslow." All of it is a revolt against accelerated living.[3]

The Slow Movement offers evidence that we really can deliberately slow down at our dinner tables, in our offices, on our roads, and in our minds. We can regain the connection and meaning that our hearts long for.

But will we?

Some of us wonder: If I grow slow, will I lose my edge? Will I lose my job? Will I miss out if I stop long enough to catch my breath?

Take heart: Growing Slow will actually make you *better* at what you do, not worse. But your focus is no longer on the pace of your growth. Instead, it's on the depth of your roots. It's walking it all out at a gospel pace, one step at a time, one task at a time, one bite at a time, one touch at a time, one conversation at a time.

We don't need to complicate this. It's the simple things that will pull us out of the culture of hurry:

Refusing to multitask, instead focusing on the single task before you.

Lighting candles at the dinner table, so you can linger with your family.

Sitting down while you eat, so you can taste the food.

Resisting the urge to check your phone at the stoplight.

Looking in their eyes—really looking—when they tell you a story.

Taking time to celebrate accomplishments, instead of flinging yourself forward to the next thing.

There's a Middle English word that, centuries ago, emerged as a way to wish someone a blessing when they were about to embark on a journey. "I wish you Godspeed."

Literally, Godspeed means, "May God cause you to succeed."

What would it look like to walk at a Godspeed pace, toward God-defined success, on our Growing Slow journey?

Godspeed is the pace of Christ. When I think of a Godspeed

pace, I think of what Eugene Peterson described in his *Message* paraphrase as the "unforced rhythms of grace."

A Godspeed pace looks like a slow walk with Jesus. Our Savior spent three years preparing his disciples for ministry; there were no life hacks for learning faster. A Godspeed pace looks like a decade or more before Paul experienced his first missionary journey. A Godspeed pace is Jesus walking, not running, along dusty roads. He passed by farm fields, taking time to draw lessons from them. He stopped at wells, paused to teach on hillsides, withdrew for long periods in the wilderness, and enjoyed long dinners with friends.

Read these verses, slowly. Let the invitation from Jesus fall gently on your weary heart.

> "Are you tired? Worn out? Burned out on religion? Come to me. Get away with me and you'll recover your life. I'll show you how to take a real rest. Walk with me and work with me—watch how I do it. Learn the unforced rhythms of grace. I won't lay anything heavy or ill-fitting on you. Keep company with me and you'll learn to live freely and lightly."[4]

The invitation is before you and me. Let's slow to the pace of Godspeed, matching step for step the unforced rhythms of days and seasons.

You don't have to hurry anymore. Your pace is *your* pace, and it will get you to the place God has prepared for you. For now, perhaps, that place is right here in your ordinary life.

Grab hold of this truth, and hold it with all your might:

God is with you in the spectacular, and he's with you in the regular. There is dignity in both places.

Your ordinary life matters. There is honor inherent in being faithful in the small things, even in the fields where the seed is just beginning to break open underground.

You don't have to be brilliant to be beautiful.

You don't have to be influential to be important.

You don't need be an authority in order to have agency over the square foot of land where our Good Lord has placed you.

He knows all about you, and he knows what's ahead. He has a plan that takes into account the mistakes you'll make, as well the little victories you ought to stop and celebrate.

God doesn't expect you to get it all right, right now.

You don't have to expect that, either.

It's time to un-hurry your heart. Growing Slow is overdue.

Some people won't like the slowed-down version of you. They'll want you to hurry up, get it right, stay the course, and keep saying *yes*. You'll confuse and frustrate them when you change your mind or when you don't "grow" fast enough. Some people won't understand you.

That's okay. They didn't plant the field that makes you, you. God did.

REMEMBER

It's okay to grow slow, because when
you grow slow, you grow deep.

REFLECT

On this freeway of life, in what areas do you worry you'll
lose your edge or "miss out" if you take the exit ramp and
head for the back roads of life?

....

....

....

Where in your life do you feel the most pressure to be
spectacular?

....

....

....

Can you recall a time in your life when you wondered if
what you were doing truly mattered?

....

....

....

Which of the symptoms on page 3 do you most relate to?
Why?

....

....

....

RETURN

At the end of each chapter,
we return to the soil.

Deep roots mattered on the farms around Colossae and in the heart of those first-generation believers. In what way do you desire deep roots in any/all of these categories?

Family

Home

Career

Faith

Recreation

Legacy

Other

CHAPTER 2

WE ARE ALL FARMERS

It is spring, the season that carries hope on feathers and in bird-song. On spring mornings, you wake up to a world that is a little bit greener and a little bit warmer, melting away the dingy gray of winter.

If you've ever planted a garden, or shopped in April for a potted arrangement for your front doorstep, you know how spring makes your spirit tingle with energy and bright optimism, like you swallowed a sunrise. Your mind swims with possibility. Dreams that hibernated all winter dare to peek their heads out once more. You shove the ice scraper far under the front seat of your car. You fantasize about the first ripe tomato.

On the farm, spring is awakened with a perennial hope. Farmers optimistically tinker with tractors and order bags of seed. Men wearing coveralls and John Deere caps gather at the local co-op, leaning their elbows on the counter while they talk about things like soil temperature and forecasts.

But this particular spring, as sheets of heavy rain assaulted the land, the farmers told a different story. In the co-op and at the cafes and the gas pumps, the farmers shook their heads, saying, "We've never had a spring quite like this."

The rains just wouldn't let up.

We're a praying community—we've got five churches in a town of 800—but we couldn't pray down a stretch of sunny days to save our lives. The window of opportunity for planting is short, so when you get a chance to enter your fields, you have to move quickly. Day after day, rain closed that window of opportunity. My husband's posture matched the posture of most farmers—hands shoved into denim pockets, shoulders drooped, eyes warily checking the western sky, which he prayed wouldn't darken. On one particularly hard day, in the midst of that incredibly hard spring, I did the only thing I knew to do. I drove along these gravel roads, and I prayed for God to move.

I call these my prayer drives, and they've helped me slow the pace and connect with God. If possible, I leave at sunrise or sunset when the cotton-candy sky is a blazing swirl of pinks and reds. A horizon like that always makes me think, *If God can throw together a sky like that, imagine what else he can do.* I turn the radio off and hear the gravel crunch beneath the tires. Silence, it seems, is rare these days. In this silence, I notice the beauty of every season: Queen Anne's lace in July, the blazing Amur maple in October, or the clouds piling up against a gunmetal-gray sky in spring.

On that spring morning, I pulled to the side of a gravel road, rolled down the window of my SUV, and snapped a picture of side-by-side unplanted fields divided by a puddled road. I opened my Facebook app, uploaded the photo, and began to type with my thumbs, while tears streamed down my cheeks:

Today, I pray for the farmers. For the skies above to be
blue. For the ground below to be dry. For equipment to
work, and for markets to flourish. And for every farmer with
a hand on a wheel to know that God truly is in control,
and that he has called them to the field—a place where we
grow more than crops, but where we also grow in faith.

I could have started this chapter with a story about a beautiful spring morning where the trees were beginning to bud, the grass beginning to green, and farmers planting first seeds into fertile ground. That will come, I promise you.

But sometimes spring looks like this: you're at the edge of your muddy field, fistfuls of seed in your hands. Here, "growth" seems like a far-off dream.

You've probably heard a sermon or seen a social media graphic that reminded you it's your job to plant the seeds, and it's God's job to make them grow. The metaphor works—that is, if you can actually plant those seeds.

But what about the fields you can't even get to? What do you do when you've been called to steward what God gave you, but you find yourself unable to fulfill the call?

Perhaps, for you, the inaccessible field looks like the heart of a wayward child who won't even text you anymore. Perhaps it's an unfulfilled dream on which someone closed a door. Perhaps you've tried to plant seeds in a flailing ministry or a fractured marriage, but you can't reach the field.

What then? What do we do when cynicism creeps up, like weeds on a bald spot of a field during a season that was designed for planting?

We will feel the urge to hurry, or busy ourselves, or try to numb the anxiety with work or food or drink. Growing Slow is an uncomfortable option when you want a fast fix.

But the secret to an un-hurried heart is found here, where the air is so quiet you can hear a faint ringing of nothingness. And all you've got is a prayer.

Seeds and Fields

In a way, we are all farmers, whether we live in a Manhattan apartment, a Houston suburb, or a California coastal city. God has given each of us seeds to plant. These seeds take the form of our daily conversations with bank tellers, toddlers, and that teenager from church you've been mentoring. These seeds are prayers, groaned into the darkness of your bedroom or at the side of a hospice bed. They look like our dreams, our work, the simple kindnesses we pour into others, our service—sometimes unnoticed. Seeds are how we spend our time and resources in a world constantly in motion. These seeds, when planted, give life meaning and purpose.

What do your seeds look like?

We, all of us, have also been given fields. These fields take the shape of our communities, our churches, our relationships, our faith journeys, our colleges, and our start-up businesses. If we are parents, the fields are the shape of our children's souls. We plant seeds, and we pray for growth. What we harvest becomes a part of our legacy, the story of our time here on earth. Even more importantly, the work of planting seeds is a mysterious partnership with the Divine.

Where, my friend, are your fields?

As it is for farmers, the planting window for your metaphorical fields can feel short. If you don't move quickly, you may worry that an opportunity will pass you by. If you're a college student, you may feel some nagging external pressure to find a mate before "the good ones are all taken." You may feel pressure to reach for a spectacular life, like I did in that college auditorium, but you are perpetually stumbling two steps behind everyone else who is killing it in every possible way. If you're a new parent, you know you have only eighteen years to instill faith in this swaddled little miracle you cradle in your arms. And if you're older, you know what it's like to be ordering her graduation gown even though the portable crib is resting against the wall in the storage closet. (Ask me how I know.)

The potential of these fields and the harvest that they might one day yield give us both our greatest joys and our greatest burdens. There is, in fact, constant pressure to grow more and better things faster. Our culture sells us hacks to help us hurry—quicker banking, faster food, workouts for time-crunched people. You may think you need all of it, because you are convinced you can't afford to slow down.

The truth is, you can't afford *not* to.

Hurry harms the human body. Your hurried heart is squeezed, and you feel it in your chest and tense shoulders. The lack of sleep. The anxiety and restlessness. You are so over it.

You want to push pause, but you don't know how.

Because fields are separated by fences, instead of walls, we can see precisely how everyone else's "crops" look. Enter the toxic sphere of comparison, which compels us to push even harder.

Who's doing better? Whose kid walked first? Who has read the Bible from cover to cover more times? Whose marriage is thriving? Who got the promotion? And whose harvest is most spectacular of all? Where I live, farmers drive along country roads in dusty pickup trucks, seeing whose crops are coming up thickest and fastest. We do the same thing, comparing ourselves to strangers on Instagram. Under the constant inspection of one another, we start to think that the people with the fastest, most impressive growth are doing it right.

How do we stop this useless comparing? How do we begin to heal our hurried hearts?

We start at the very beginning, on Earth's first farm.

The First Farm Was a Paradise

This desire to plant seeds and grow good things is hardwired into us.

Our story, after all, begins with a divine farmer, pushing seeds into dirt.

Now the LORD God had planted a garden.[1]

The Garden of Eden was the ultimate farm, perfect in every

way—no strife, disease, heartbreak, cancer, sadness, abuse, or broken relationships. Earth's first humans didn't have to worry about drought or flooding. The perfect amount of mist rose from the ground to water the earth. Flowers stretched tall, swiveling their faces toward the sun. Birds flitted from branch to budding branch. Imagine strolling the grounds in the cool of the day with God, admiring it all, anticipating the harvest, and later, taking a bite, wide-eyed when you taste perfection.

Like the Lord, Adam was a farmer.

> The Lord God took the man and put him in the Garden of Eden to work it and take care of it.[2]

Where I live, I often see dads farming side by side with their sons or daughters. When I do, I imagine the joy Adam must have felt farming with his Father.

When Adam wasn't planting seeds, his Father assigned him the fun task of naming the animals.

> He brought them to the man to see what he would name them.[3]

Don't you love that? God could have named the animals himself, but he gave the job to Adam, letting him participate in the creative aspects of this Edenic farm. I have no way of knowing, of course, but I imagine a smile stretching across the Lord's face when Adam came up with names like *pleasing fungus beetle, pink fairy armadillo, raspberry crazy ant, frill-necked lizard.* (Yes, these are real names of animals. I didn't cross-check the Greek or anything, but I found them all on the internet, so they must be accurate.)

Paradise was short-lived. Sin barreled into the world, delivering with it the first Farm Crisis. The cause: Adam and Eve ate from the only tree from which they were forbidden to eat. Adam and Eve struggled with an underlying problem: we should be more or do more. For humanity's first couple, that urge led them to eat forbidden fruit, to "be like God."[4] It wasn't enough that they had every other tree available to them. They wanted something more. They were cast out from that first farm, "to work the ground from which (Adam) had been taken."[5]

The urge that led Adam and Eve to sin is the same kind of urge that infects our lives. It leads to hurry, exhaustion, and eventually, frantic living. We're trying to do the right things, grow good things, but we feel like God isn't cooperating. He seems like a slow God. So we look for hacks and systems to move our priorities forward.

The whole of Scripture happens between two farms—the Edenic farm of Genesis and the restored Edenic farm of Revelation. Until we reach the restored Eden—a place with no more tears and no more sadness—we exist in this in-between place. Between two farms, we sow seeds of joy, but we also sow seeds of sorrow. We face heartache, disappointment, and a longing to see good fruit come up from this old ground.

Our story, with its fields and seeds, plays out in this in-between place. We are like the roaming Israelites, longing for a promised land that flows with milk and honey. We hold on to God's oath that it's coming:

> "For the LORD your God is bringing you into a good land—a
> land with brooks, streams, and deep springs gushing out into
> the valleys and hills; a land with wheat and barley, vines and
> fig trees, pomegranates, olive oil and honey."[6]

For the Israelites, the journey toward the promised land took forty years. It was, indeed, a Growing Slow journey—maybe even a little un-spectacular as months turned into years. Those forty years were filled with God's promises, but also with great periods of doubt and discouragement.

Here's why all of that biblical backstory matters:

In a Growing Slow journey, God meets us in the in-between, un-spectacular places. He provides and protects and holds fast to his promises.

For the Israelites, this slow, wandering journey was the place they came to know God most of all. The Lord revealed himself as someone who would never leave them, who would provide manna, water, and the surprise of quail. In their Growing Slow walk through the wilderness, God never left their side.

And he'll never leave ours.

Where are you, my friend? As you roam between the first farm of Genesis and the final farm of Revelation, where do you find yourself? What's the lay of the land before you?

Perhaps your "crops" are growing up thick and tall, and you see God's goodness in the land of milk and honey. In these fields, pause to thank him for his provision.

Or perhaps you can't access your fields, and you feel like you're in a wilderness, wandering around like an Israelite. Sometimes you will want to give in or give up. But God is working in ways we can't even see. Just as God never left his people in the wilderness, he won't abandon you, either.

"My presence will go with you, and I will give you rest."[7]

The First Step to Healing a Hurried Heart

Almost every morning that particular spring, I paused at the front window of our house. It affords us the view of a single field's gentle slope, rolling out from the yard's edge and down toward the county blacktop road.

Standing in this spot grounds me. It connects me to the land, to the generations who've farmed these acres before us, to my neighbors—whom I recognize by their tractors and pickup trucks—and to a God who loves playing in the dirt.

Some mornings, the fog hangs low and feathery over the fields just beyond the blacktop road. To me, when the fog fills the valley like that, it looks like the sky dropped down to kiss the earth.

The steam from my coffee curls. A robin flits to perch upon a high branch of a tree. Leaves, newly unfurled at the command of spring, are shimmering in dappled morning light. Paying attention like this is a way of Growing Slow. It helps me see that the land is not only beautiful, but also filled with great purpose—because God made it so.

Today, I think of you and what you're growing in your fields. Growth is slow work, isn't it? Sometimes it takes time—even years—before you see it. Planting seeds, without seeing results right away, is the hard work called *faith*. In faith, your knees have been dirtied. In faith, you have mud under your fingernails. In faith, you've left footprints in those fields. This can't be hurried, no matter how much this world makes you think you're falling behind.

The secret to healing your hurried heart begins with step one: holding onto hope as if your life depends on it.

Hurry wounds a hope-filled heart. Christ, in turn, will heal it.

I don't say this because I think it's true. I say it because God promised. Because of Jesus, we have a "living hope,"[8] not a dead hope. Biblical hope is a confident expectation. It is the full assurance that God is going to come through as we press seeds into the dirt.

Slow down today and let the living hope of a living God engulf you.

As we move through the seasons of Growing Slow, let's plant our feet firmly in the fields of perennial hope. Let's remind ourselves of God's promise and provision. Let's refuse to rush through seasons of our lives, for God is making everything beautiful in its time. There really is a time for everything, and maybe not every season gives you exactly what you want, but slowly, in his time, God unfolds his plan for all that we plant.

It takes great courage to hope. But we can do this. We can wake up each day and stand at the window with hope.

A single bit of hope is a very powerful thing. It compels you to look out on your fields, believing that they will open up for you once more.

Until then, cast your seeds where you can. Wait for the time to enter the now-fallow fields. Never minimize the living hope given to you, in the name of the One who placed the fields before you.

I pray that we would take the time we need to let hope do its work within us. Hope has a warrior quality, and in an age of cynicism and disbelief, it will give us the courage to grow slow. Hope sees to it that we will not cave to the pressure of immediacy. Our hope isn't in benchmarks or speed or prominence; it's in the God of seasons and seeds and rain and dirt.

Take the time you need here, seed planter.

Take the time you need to study your fields. Take the time you need to make that decision about the job, the move, the relationship, the college.

Take the time you need to explore all the options.

Take the time you need to rest and pray.

You are a farmer, even if you don't grow literal seeds in literal fields. You are planting seeds of hopes and dreams, praying for a bit of growth here and there.

> "This is what the kingdom of God is like. A man scatters seed
> on the ground. Night and day, whether he sleeps or gets up,
> the seed sprouts and grows, *though he does not know how.*"[9]

Do you see it there? God is doing the work, not us. Find peace in knowing that, under the dirt, Earth's first Farmer is already growing good things.

REMEMBER

Hurry wounds a hope-filled heart.
Christ, in turn, will heal it.

REFLECT

How have you felt the hopefulness of spring, only to see
those hopes dashed?

....
....

Where have you seen life spring forth, or are you still in a
season of waiting?

....
....
....

Do you ever feel like you're running out of time, like you
need to create some kind of legacy? If so, how?

....
....
....

How does comparison make it especially difficult to
"grow slow"?

....
....
....

RETURN

At the end of each chapter,
we return to the soil.

Perhaps you are in a season where you feel like the growth in your soil is especially slow. Name your frustration. What is God saying to you in this season?

....

....

....

....

....

....

....

....

....

....

....

....

....

....

....

....

....

....

....

....

....

CHAPTER 3

WE ARE ALSO FIELDS

In the rush to grow good things in our fields, we overlook the
most important growth of all: the blooming inside of *us* as God
tends to *our* souls.

Yes, we are all absolutely farmers, planting seeds in people and
places. But let's not miss this: we are also fields, dirt in the hands
of God, who breathes life and love into each of us.

Behold:

You are God's field.[1]

The Bible is a really big book, and for the first time in my life,
I am reading it cover to cover in a year. That's an embarrassing
confession when you consider the fact that I have been in Christian
women's ministry for many years. At the start of this year, our older
daughter, Lydia, handed me a printed sheet of daily readings and
asked if I would accept her challenge to read the whole Bible in a
year; she planned to do the same. I am so happy I said yes. It has
been one of the most enlightening journeys through Scripture I
have ever undertaken. Scripture has come alive for me in a whole
new way.

This journey through the Bible has awakened me to the fact that I too often use Scripture as a way to find an answer to a personal problem, or to glean a teaching that I can later share with you on my social media, in a keynote address, or in a book. That's not all bad, of course, but what I have rarely done in recent years is approach the text merely as a love letter from an intimate God who actually enjoys watching me grow.

Nearly every page of Scripture reveals what God cares about— and what he doesn't care about—as he grows us into maturity. This is what I'm learning anew:

We don't have to be the "next big thing." We don't have to be the ladder climber or the one in the spotlight to grow great things. Repeatedly, Jesus reminds us that God exalts the lowly and humbles the proud. He is not impressed by status or by "the strength of a horse or . . . human might."[2] God is not looking to build up spiritual VIPs with long, right-sounding prayers.[3] Nor has he endorsed the Christian celebrity culture that entices with its siren of fame.

He isn't growing us into superstars; he's growing us into servants.

Growing Slow is a school of patience in which we are nurtured into spiritual maturity. Growing Slow is a daily choice to see where God is already working and then the conscious decision to join him there. Sometimes it's heavy and it's hard and the rain won't let up for a second. But instead of running from the rain, you need to step right out in it, letting it wash your eyes so you aren't blind to the beauty that's still here.

And it is. It's still here.

Growing Slow is the belief that Christ is our only hope, that heaven is our future home, and that we have been given the wondrous privilege of planting in Earth's precious fields—both literal and metaphorical—before we go to an Edenic farm someday.

You can't chart the way of Growing Slow on a spreadsheet.

Stories of spectacular growth in businesses or ministries earn accolades and trophies at banquets for the Who's Who and the so-and-so's. But how are unseen and internal milestones rewarded? Probably less like a framed certificate and more like a "prize for which God has called me heavenward in Christ Jesus."[4]

Deliberately choosing to grow slow means we will be less concerned with the kind of growth that this world fixates on. Numbers don't define us and won't rule us when we develop a Growing Slow mindset. Peter tells us the kind of growth that matters most is the growth happening on the inside: "Grow in grace and understanding of our Master and Savior, Jesus Christ."[5]

The most important growth of all, personal transformation, happens slowly.

We ourselves are slow grown, like these crops in my husband's fields.

Can I show you?

Each spring, on the first day of planting, I am like a child, running to the field, surrendered wholly to the beauty of new beginnings.

You must know this: I am not like the other farm wives here. I don't know a lick about hog futures or the mechanics of a planter. You may think that I'm over here with a flour-dusted apron, baking bread and feeding baby cows and scooping eggs out from under chickens like a regular Laura Ingalls Wilder.

I don't know a lot of things. But I *do* know beauty when I see it.

I do know that when I walk the rows of these fields, or through the tree grove out back, all of the most beautiful things were slow grown. I do know how to make my husband's favorite kind of sandwich, toss it in a sack, and bring it to the field. I do run down crop rows, sack swinging beside me, then I climb up the steps on the John Deere to sit next to Scott as he drops corn seeds into the straightest rows. He's got one hand on the wheel, and with the other he holds his sandwich. And the guy I fell in love with during his first year of law school is now talking to me about soybean aphids and the cost of fertilizer.

He'll plant millions of seeds, burying them down in the dark. And for many days—sometimes even weeks—we'll see nothing.

No growth.

No evidence of the miracle of life that is happening beneath our feet.

And then, one morning, we'll wake up to the tiniest shoots of green. As the old saying goes, the corn will be "knee high by the Fourth of July," and most likely much taller. Before long, tassels are waving in the breeze, signaling pollination.

Day to day, the growth is nearly imperceptible. But it happens! Growth happens, slowly, until one day, you realize that you have to tip your chin toward the sky to see the tops of the corn tassels.

You and I aren't corn plants, of course, but we are grown slowly, too. Sometimes the day-to-day growth is imperceptible. But I have to believe it's happening.

I have to believe God designed us to develop spiritual maturity and obedience over time. It seems to me that God is interested in incremental growth as we develop habits of obedience, deep trust, and holiness. If that wasn't the case, we would have all been born as fully formed adults, with robust faith and matured trust already intact. Instead, we come into this world as babies, learning over time, through struggles, and in the midst of disappointment what it truly means to trust Jesus.

Often, I have wondered why my maturity and growth takes so long.

Why this slow growth, Lord, why? Lord, you have the ability to bring me to full maturity.

So why do I grow so painfully slow?

Perhaps the answer is simply this: the Farmer who planted seeds within us enjoys the beauty that emerges when we simply grow slow.

Growing Slow Begins with a Choice

I made my choice to grow slow—and to be grown slow.

I made it because I didn't want to be the kind of mom who misses her daughter's one-minute moment to shine on the court because I was answering an email from a women's conference leader. I didn't want to be the kind of friend who isn't fully present when we're out for dinner. I didn't want to be the kind of woman who devalued her own life when I compared it to someone whose follower count is exploding on Instagram. I no longer wanted to dismiss the quotidian and unseen moments because of external pressure to dream a bigger dream.

Jesus meets me in ordinary ways that are so specific, so personal: when a giant moon lights up the blackest night, when a ripened tomato calls to me from the vine, when a neighbor waves across the field. This is life! The smell of sautéing onions and garlic filling the room; catching fireflies with my bare hands; pouring wine for guests; hanging out with the kids on the deck, wrapped in fleece blankets, while we leave our phones inside on the counter. It's the new litter of baby kittens that arrive every spring, always plotting mischief in the barn. It's the sack lunches I pack for Scott. It's the potluck at church, where the kitchen hums with Crock-Pots and ovens set at 350 degrees, warming pounds of meatloaf and lasagna in Pyrex beds. You know I'm always going to bring the corn casserole, its top sprinkled with those crispy French-fried onions that come in a can. Grandma Joyce, Scott's mom, will bring the chicken and wild rice soup.

A life of connection is what I desire—connecting to others, but also connecting to *me*. Simple, unique, down-to-earth me who makes casseroles from canned goods, who drives a muddy car, who doesn't know the difference between a designer purse and a cheap knockoff.

I am as regular as they come. But you know what?

I am growing good things in my life. Even more importantly, God is growing regular *me*.

I am God's field, and so are you. You are exactly where you are supposed to be, under the right kind of sky for this particular moment in history, set out for you from the beginning of time. God knows the lay of the land that makes you *you*. He is planting seeds within you—seeds which will bear internal fruit with eternal value.

He knows exactly how to care for you, cultivate you, and grow you.

Our Father says you're a field. And his Son says you are like soil.

In the parable of seeds and soil, Jesus is the sower. He plants his seeds in all of us, but what grows depends on the condition of the soil. The Bible says there are four types of soil: impenetrable, shallow, thorny, and good.

It's pretty clear which soil type is most desirable—the good soil. But can I be straight with you? I have been all four kinds of soil in my life. I wish I could tell you I've only been a Good Soil Girl, but that's not true. My heart has been as hard as a rock, as thorny as a cactus patch, and as shallow as soup on a saucer. Let me give you a brief tour of my side-switching heart with its temperamental soil:

My impenetrable soil: God planted seeds in the soil of my heart that, quite frankly, couldn't take root. I was self-reliant, disillusioned, confused, and drawing my worth from past achievements. But God relentlessly pursued me; he kept right on planting.

My shallow soil: There have been moments in my spiritual journey when I experienced the ecstasy of hearing God speak directly to my heart, though this heart be two-faced and demanding. I have felt his presence and specific kindness as he scattered seeds unabated upon this shallow soil. But because I was who I was, the seed planted in this soil was the equivalent of a brief, Bible camp high: fulfilling for a moment but lacking fruit that lasts. I didn't have the courage to be committed. I was fickle and selfish. I ended up sun-scorched because of those shallow roots. "There is no soil of character, and so when the emotion wears off and some difficulty arrives, there is nothing to show for it."[6]

Good grief, I've been a mess, haven't I?

Still, God kept planting.

My thorny soil: In other seasons, God planted his seeds into the thorniest, prickliest parts of me. I received his Word and direction, but my train-wreck self choked out the growth he intended. I rushed for approval and attention. I acted on impulse, afraid of falling behind or losing my edge.

But, still, God kept planting in me.

Are you seeing the pattern here?

God won't stop planting in you, either.

Do you see how hopelessly in love with us he is? We are so much more than our shallow, stubborn, disillusioned, insecure, or prickly selves. We are fields that a divine Farmer refuses to give up on! Let's not confuse the state of our soil with the mysterious, unrelenting affection of a God who loves to watch us grow.

This is unconditional love and acceptance—that God keeps planting.

In his persistence, God won't stop planting until he finds our good soil, "produced a harvest beyond his wildest dreams."[7]

The harvest beyond our wildest dreams doesn't look like a promotion or a spotlight.

The harvest beyond our wildest dreams is simply this: the fingerprints of a loving God upon our souls. You and I bear the mark of having been planted with purpose by a God who won't give up on us. We may have to wait until heaven to know what harvest will come of the fields where we roam and where we plant.

As long as there is soil, God is always planting. He refuses to see you as anything less than a field worth tending, and he is willing to grow slow with us. This is his outrageous love. This is his Growing Slow way. Before he grows good things *through* us, he wants to grow good things *in* us.

> "These things I plan won't happen right away. Slowly, steadily, surely, the time approaches when the vision will be fulfilled. If it seems slow, do not despair, for these things will surely come to pass. Just be patient! They will not be overdue a single day!"[8]

It's okay to slow it all down, to dial back expectations, and to open yourself up to God's impeccable timing and his unrelenting patience. *"These things will surely come to pass."*

I don't know what's growing in your life today. I don't know what areas of growth seem unimpressive. I don't know the condition of your soil. But I do know that God is growing you through it.

Keep going. Keep growing.

There's an Ancient Way to guide us.

REMEMBER

He refuses to see you as anything
less than a field worth tending, and
he is willing to grow slow with us.

REFLECT

As you consider growth in your life, has your focus been
on external growth or internal growth?

....

....

....

How can a Growing Slow mindset help you keep
your eyes fixed on internal growth and personal
transformation?

....

....

....

....

As you consider your own spiritual growth, does it seem
that God has grown you quickly or slowly?

....

....

....

....

RETURN

At the end of each chapter,
we return to the soil.

Have you always been good soil? Or has your life also been marked by moments of impenetrability, shallowness, and thorniness? Use the timeline below, representing your life, to mark periods of soil quality. Indicate years or seasons at the hashmarks. Below the timeline, in the space provided, name the "soil" of your heart at that point in your life history. Perhaps you could take note of the circumstances or events that affected the quality of the soil in your heart.

Write year or
season here.

Soil type
and life
circumstances
here.

CHAPTER 4

THE ANCIENT WAY OF
GROWING SLOW

The Ancient Way of Growing Slow is both beautiful and awful. I'm telling you, it will break your heart, and then it will be the only way you know that hope is still alive in this devastating, wonderful place called Earth.

The Ancient Way is filled with both natural rhythms and dizzying surprises; dark rooms, and then lights flickering in the hallway, like hope. You will cry in the shower, and then you will cry a different way when you stand at the first notes of "Pomp and Circumstance." The tears will taste the same both times, but your soul will know the difference between them.

You will think you've been forgotten, but later, you will know you had been held the whole time.

In the middle of it, you will be certain that this Ancient Way will wreck you, but along comes the most jaw-dropping promise: in time, every single thing will be made beautiful.

The Ancient Way, you see, has always been this:

For everything there is a season, and a time for every
    matter under heaven:
a time to be born, and a time to die;
a time to plant, and a time to pluck up what is planted;
a time to kill, and a time to heal;
a time to break down, and a time to build up;
a time to weep, and a time to laugh;
a time to mourn, and a time to dance;
a time to cast away stones, and a time to gather stones
    together;
a time to embrace, and a time to refrain from embracing;
a time to seek, and a time to lose;
a time to keep, and a time to cast away;
a time to tear, and a time to sew;
a time to keep silence, and a time to speak;
a time to love, and a time to hate;
a time for war, and a time for peace.[1]

You will want to run away from the unknowability of it all. You
will want to turn to drink, or food, or accomplishment, or Amazon
Prime to neurotically avoid it. The human will does not easily bend
to such a plan, which calls you to accept whatever comes your way.

But stay here. Be fully present. In each season, you will find
that the secret to Growing Slow comes in the waiting as the Lord
plants seeds into the precious, yielding soil of you. In this place,
tucked under the dirt, you will grow roots deep enough to push
forth the fruit of a life worth living.

He has made everything beautiful in its time.[2]

But What If the Ancient Way Scares Us?

Confession time.

I am afraid of the Ancient Way, because I am afraid of pain. I am afraid of losing control and of falling behind while other people achieve what I have only dreamed of.

In secret places, I have darker fears.

My one recurring fear is death, but there it sits in the middle of the Ancient Way of Growing Slow: "a time to die."

A friend's grandfather always told her that he wanted to die well, because you only get one chance to do it. He wanted to die with grace and humor and hope, loving the people around him until the last possible second. That's exactly how it turned out for him. I'm afraid that I won't die well. Chances are, I'll be the crabby, delirious woman losing her mind and seeing unicorns moving in the wallpaper. Or I'll make it really hard for the people I leave behind because of some dumb thing I said in the stupor of pain before they gave me the morphine.

I am afraid of so many things about life—of being abandoned or betrayed. Of being unable to control my emotions or having horrible things happen to my kids. Some people have to go through really hard seasons, much harder than mine have been, and I don't know how I would ever deal with those.

Theologically, I know that God is in the business of making all the bad things come untrue. I believe in redemption and beauty from ashes.

But we haven't reached that restored Edenic farm just yet. We are living in the already and the not yet. Our eternal future is secure, but we haven't reached the destination.

I'm nervous and ill-equipped for all the things I don't know that are supposed to be a bridge from my theological knowledge of eternity to my everyday life right now.

I confess that I don't always believe "Jesus is enough" for whatever season of the Ancient Way I'm in. I *say* I believe it. But I don't always live those words in a whole-hearted way. That sobering reality brought me to my knees one afternoon, when I was singing along to a song about Jesus being more than enough for every thirst and every need.

The song played on, but I stopped singing.

Because did I really believe that? Did I really believe that God is "more than enough"?

Do I hustle and push because I have to fill in perceived gaps in God's plans for my life? Do I resist the invitation to grow slow because I'm afraid of the divine reliance and blind trust it requires? Do I value external growth more than the work God is doing inside me?

Could I sing of Jesus' enough-ness if something awful happened to my kids? If my marriage fell apart? If we couldn't afford all the stuff I love so much? If I lost my ability to reason or write? If I lost the will to dream or hope?

These questions make me uncomfortable. And the older I get, the more I am challenged to grapple with them, because as you age, the harder halves of the verses in Ecclesiastes 3 eventually all come true. I have lived long enough to feel the grief, the dying, the weeping, and the losing.

Someday, either my husband or I will grieve the loss of the other. Our daughters won't need me like they need me now. As I age, I could lose my memory and even my ability to remember the names of my own children.

Yes, I am afraid.

Yet I also desire to know deeply that everything I have is because of him and that all I have is more than I deserve. I am certain that I'll know, when I get to heaven, how true it is: Jesus really is enough. But I don't want to wait until I'm standing before my Savior to believe it with my whole heart.

This faith asks me to embrace the uncomfortable-ness of changing seasons as well as fields that seem unfruitful at the moment.

We all want the fruit, right? We want the healing, and the building up, and the love, and the keeping that God offers in Ecclesiastes 3. We don't really want the weeping and the losing and, by all means, the killing.

I don't want the seed in the ground to die. Yet it must. There is no life without the dying.

Jesus said, "I can guarantee this truth. A single grain of wheat doesn't produce anything unless it is planted in the ground and dies. If it dies, it will produce a lot of grain."[3]

Our will must die. Our desire to rush through hard seasons must die. Our belief that we're in charge here must die. Our demands. Our misguided plans. Our selfish ambitions. All of it must die.

If the seed dies, the fruit grows, Jesus says.

I have seen evidence of fruit from slow, deep growth. I've seen the beautiful ways that seeds we planted long ago, grown slow, are now bearing fruit in our marriage, our children, our home. Just this morning, our oldest daughter sat at the kitchen table, filling out her daily prayer journal, a practice that, she tells me, she picked up from me when I didn't even know she was paying attention.

Yes, there has been growth, out in these fields, and inside our hearts and home. There has been laughter. There has also been weeping.

In this year of writing through the seasons of Growing Slow, pain was a steady companion, holding hands with joy. Even here, I trust that God will make everything beautiful in its time.

Walk, and Not Faint

From the back of the convention center, the teacher dialed my husband's number. The news she delivered was alarming: In that very moment, our daughter lay, unresponsive, at her feet at a leadership convention, wearing a red blazer and her first-ever pair of black heels. We had bought them the week before.

Scott and I were at a musical contest many miles away with our other daughter. He turned white, motioned me out of the auditorium, and put the phone on speaker so I could hear. I listened to the teacher's words coming through the phone, but I couldn't really understand what she was saying. What I *could* hear was my heart crashing against my chest; it pulsed in my ears, hot.

"Anna. She passed out," the teacher said again. "The ambulance is on the way."

I met them at the emergency room. By then, they had taken blood and administered fluids through an IV. Maybe Anna was just nervous about whether she'd advance to the next level of competition, the nurses said. Maybe she hadn't had enough water. She was a little dehydrated. So, yeah, maybe.

The doctor dismissed our daughter from the ER with a reminder to drink plenty of fluids. We left, satisfied with the answer and grateful it was nothing worse.

The next day, she passed out again.

And then the day after that.

There were scans, heart monitors, more blood drawn, more theories postulated. One specialist said it was a virus. Another said anxiety or stress. Most said passing out was actually common among teens, and that she'd "grow out of it." It was generally agreed-upon that she has a weak immune system which doesn't play nice with her nervous system.

For a couple of weeks in the spring, she was in a wheelchair at school. Granted, it was a safer place to be than on her own two feet in the event that she did pass out again. We worried that if she passed out, she would hit her head on a desk or the locker room floor. And she did pass out again. And again. Her legs were weak, anyway. So the wheelchair it was.

Those were the days when I cried in the shower.

But there was also laughing. We laughed hard, especially on the day when Anna came up with a great idea. "Let's pass out treats to thank all the teachers who have been helping me," she said, and we laughed because of the double meaning of "pass out treats."

There were some people who couldn't grasp our macabre sense of humor during those times, why we'd joke about something so serious, but sometimes laughing about what hurt was how we coped.

That spring, I drove Anna to school instead of putting her on the bus. Each morning, I lifted her wheelchair into the back of our Explorer. And off we went, down the country lane, tracing the rural roads to the school, which sits out in the middle of farm fields. It's the same school her dad attended a generation earlier.

Ever since the girls have been able to speak, I've prayed with them most mornings, after breakfast and before school. One morning, on the way to school with the wheelchair in the back, our prayers focused on Anna's need for healing and for us to embrace what God wanted to show us through the difficulty of this season. Anna insisted that fruit would come from this, even as I quietly doubted. Ah, the faith of a child.

That morning, God seemed to provide just the verse we needed, as he often does. I prayed Scripture that I now believe God divinely brought to mind: "Lord, I pray that Anna would soar on wings like eagles, that she would run and not grow weary, that she would walk and not faint."

It was with those final words—"Walk and not faint"—that Anna and I turned our heads to face each other. Amazed, I pulled the Explorer over to the side of the road and took in the applicability of these verses. I had pondered that passage numerous times, but never, in all my life, had I prayed them so literally.

It was so wondrously rich that I actually laughed out loud. "Anna!" I said. "Did you hear that? Walk and not faint?"

"Yes! I did, Mom. I did!" She was as giddy as I was. She opened up a Bible app on her phone and read the verses aloud.

"Anna," I said. "We can pray those verses until God carries us through this season."

And that's what we did. We prayed Isaiah 40:31, but we prayed it backward, to follow the progression of Anna's required healing: that she would walk and not faint, that she would run without weariness, and finally, that she would soar.

In time, the fainting subsided. Within weeks, she was running on the track team. She ran, did not grow weary, and at times, it seemed like she was soaring around that track.

It's been difficult to tell this story because of unexpected emotional hurts that have accompanied Anna's health problems, and because it has felt like a long journey toward healing. One of the most heartbreaking parts of the journey came about as a result of anonymous cyberbullying and cruel remarks from other children, who accused Anna of faking her illness when her symptoms persisted.

Some nights, I have been awakened from my sleep by shame—shame for not being able to shield my child from pain, shame for not knowing the answers to questions people ask, shame for feeling shame when I know better.

The physical healing came slowly. The emotional healing has been even slower. And let me be frank: we don't want to "grow slow" in this. We want fast progress.

But some seasons don't pass quickly, so we had to sit in the mourning and the weeping, believing with all that is in us that we would see restoration.

My friend Anjuli reminds me that heartbreaks like these are compounded when you don't have a category to put them in or a name to give them. She puts these kind of heartbreaks in the "bad things that happened" box. She wrote about it in her book, *Stay*:

We each have a trauma, or a "bad thing that happened": an accident, a death, a disapproving father, an angry mother, an illness, a pastor who failed you, a divorce, a coach who shamed you, a friend who left you, a boy who hurt you, a miscarriage that wrecked you. No matter how horrible or small and painful or disgusting it was, stop running from it. Stop pretending it's okay or isn't there because that trauma is going to bury you in lies . . . Stop running. I beg of you. Sit down. Stay.[4]

The Ancient Way of Growing Slow calls us to sit down and stay. The plan both grounds us and confounds us; it keeps us sane and drives us crazy. But as Anjuli says, we must stay with it.

Sometimes the fruit of Growing Slow comes in the harvest of your public fields, but sometimes it is grown in the privacy of your own heart.

The Ancient Way doesn't provide easy answers or solutions. Sometimes, it raises more questions than answers.

For instance, look closely at Ecclesiastes 3:3—"a time to kill and a time to heal." What kind of plan is this? Kill is, quite simply, a hard word. Say it out loud once. Even if you try to say it sweetly, you end up sounding like a psychopath.

This ancient line from this ancient plan is not the sort of verse you will find slapped on a coffee mug at your local Christian bookstore, but there it sits in our Bibles, and I wrestle with it. Our world and its history are pocked with the anguish of killing and sickness and pain.

There is a time for everything. *Everything.* That's the simple, complicated truth about this broken, paradoxical earth—marked alternately by killing and healing and life and death and joy and pain and sorrow and celebration. The brokenness shatters us in places like hospitals and funeral homes and battlefields and a teenage girl's bedroom when she can't find her happy ending. We are left to grapple with it.

How does the Ancient Way sit with you today?

What dream has been killed? What loss has been mourned? When have you wanted to embrace, but instead had to keep your distance, waiting until the Lord at last says, "It's time! Embrace!" Where have you felt shame? What is inside your "bad thing that happened" box? What season has wrecked you?

There's more.

Where have you seen the healing? Where have you felt the joy? What growth are you just now beginning to see where you took the bravest move of all: letting the seed die?

Life is hard, but it's also beautiful.

It's all being made beautiful in the hands of God. In his time.

Let's keep our eyes open in these seasons when we want to shut ourselves off from it all. Don't run away or hide. Grow slow, friend.

For my part, I will stubbornly choose to believe that God is working things out in his way, his timing.

I don't have a perfect and happy ending for this chapter. This one falls in Anjuli's "bad things that happened" box, and I can't tie a bow around that box. But I think there's dirt at the bottom of the box, and even there, good things will grow.

REMEMBER

Sometimes the fruit of Growing Slow
comes in the harvest of your public
fields, but sometimes it is grown in
the privacy of your own heart.

REFLECT

Reread the verses from Ecclesiastes 3 on page 40, about
what I call the Ancient Way. What part of the Ancient
Way scares you most?

....

....

....

As the Ancient Way unfolds in your life, where has
shame been a companion?

....

....

....

Which part of the Ancient Way are you living in right
now—the planting, healing, and embracing parts, or the
weeping, mourning, and tearing parts? Perhaps you have
one foot in two seasons.

....

....

....

RETURN

At the end of each chapter, we return to the soil.

What's inside your "bad thing that happened" box? How does it change things to know that there might be soil at the bottom of the box? Write a prayer to God, telling him your desires for the things you've tucked away in that box.

CHAPTER 5

LETTING GO OF EXPECTATIONS

I 've been a plan maker my whole life.

That's why it's a challenge for me to embrace the Ancient Way. I pray, "Thy will be done," but I often prefer my will.

This preference dictated my grow-fast life. It dictated where I would rent an apartment, how I would parent, which jobs I would take, how I wouldn't allow my heart to be broken, when I'd give in to change, and when I would flat-out refuse. I operated as if I were the CEO of my life, and God was an employee.

I've had stubborn expectations, which can be a beautiful thing when I'm partnering with God but a painful thing when I demand my own way. Or when those expectations shatter into a million pieces to make the mosaic that is my life.

I am certain you know what I mean, but if your life has gone exactly as planned, you are free to skip this chapter.

If my words ring true, join me here at this crossroads: the place where my will meets God's will.

This is the land of a million un-expectations.

For this land, I can honestly thank God today, even with tears stinging my eyes at the remembrance of loss.

For the sudden moves and the job changes I never wanted.

For love lost and for love found.

Even for heartaches and harvests that greatly disappointed us. I thank God for these, because, in the suffering most of all, I came to know God. In the pain, I encountered the balm of Gilead. I discovered the courage to love the ordinary, boring parts of life, along with the detours that brought me where I am today.

And thank the good Lord above that he had the nerve to say "no" to so many of my most earnest prayers, uttered from the heart of great expectation. If my earliest prayers were answered, I would have married the wrong guy. I would have landed that incredible reporting job I'd been eyeing, and would have deteriorated fully into the cynical, ascerbic, and frustrated person I was slowly becoming. I would have had all the New York subway routes memorized. Instead, I get to wake up in a bright house at the end of country lane. An unexpected life is not the same as a bad life.

A Growing Slow life can be both disruptive and magnificent at the same time.

My oldest sister always cautioned me against expectation. She told me that we can't handle seeing too far ahead in this life, that our minds simply can't deal with the pressure of what's around the bend.

My plan-tastic personality largely resisted her admonitions. Now I understand.

If I knew too much about what was to come, I would have resisted and manipulated. I would have rushed through the seasons that hurt the most, rather than staying in the rearranged places where God chose to come close. In my race for the comforts the world offers, I would have missed the blessed comfort of my Christ.

I need this comfort, not only in the harsh swirling of a winter squall, but in the spring.

Doorways and Tulips

I've had a lifelong love affair with spring, but where I live, it always feels like the shortest season of the year—and the most unpredictable. You get a hint of spring—tiny buds appearing on slender branches, birds winging north again—then a late-season snowstorm will strike, hiding everything under a white duvet.

People here joke that if you don't like the weather, wait a day. And it's true. Many times, we've been hit with an April snow, only to watch it melt the very next day under a sun so bright you have to put the visor down when you drive.

Spring will give you whiplash, but it remains my favorite. It smells like dirt and feels like the healing hand of God, who decided to give everyone a great, big do-over.

It's the season that makes me feel most hopeful.

I think that's why the spring of 2008 never felt like spring at all—even during the planting season, when farmers revved up the tractor engines. My father-in-law was diagnosed with leukemia a few weeks before the first tulips popped open their glossy mouths. The cancer was presumed to have been caused by his exposure decades earlier to Agent Orange, a herbicide used to clear trees during the Vietnam War.

This diagnosis would have never been on our list of expectations. Scott planned to farm these fields alongside his father, Paul, for many years, just as Paul had done until Grandpa Milo died at age ninety-five. Just as Milo had done with his father Ole, who was born at the end of the post-Civil War Reconstruction Era, and lived to age eighty-three. Those Lee genes are hearty.

Our daughters were six and three at the time of the leukemia diagnosis. They immediately asked us if "Bop"—as they called him—was going to die. The prognosis wasn't good, but there were treatments to take, prayers to pray, moments to be brave, days to be lived—one precious hour at a time.

We told the girls how dying isn't a dead end but a doorway.

And until we got to the doorway, we had a lot of living to do in the hallway. I still remember all the tea parties Bop hosted on the deck of their farmhouse that year. He would sit cross-legged in his Levis and dirty work boots. The cups were dainty in his big farmer hands.

Spring bloomed. And many weeks after the diagnosis, the girls and I were walking through a park, where gardeners had tended to rows of tulips for an annual tulip festival. We didn't get to the park during the tulips' prime blooming days. By the time we showed up, the tulips' heads had begun to nod, their color fading.

We knelt down by the dying flowers. The girls cupped the soft petals in their small hands. I told them how the tulips were perennials.

"They bloom every single year, but just for a little while. Then they fade, and the petals fall off, and it looks like they are dying. But next spring, these same tulips will bloom again."

The younger daughter asked me, "Why are you crying, Mommy? Are you crying because we got here too late?" And I just hugged them and told them how beautiful the flowers were, even when they were dying.

Summer came. Bop grew weaker, and we all felt a shift in our prayers toward accepting things we couldn't change.

Fall arrived in a streak of gold, and Bop willed his weak self to work alongside his son on the farm, taking turns on the combine or pulling grain wagons into town with the tractor. It would be his last harvest, and I remembered how, though they were frail, his hands still looked so big.

By December, Bop was bald and in a hospital room. We tried to cheer him with presents and Santa hats on Christmas Day. The nurses created one of those pain charts where you rate how much you hurt based on a scale of 1–10 by using Santas wearing red hats and various stages of emotion on their faces.

The sad Santas looked the way we felt.

Carols played on a radio down the hall. Life kept right on going, despite all this dying.

By January, well before the tulips would bloom again, Bop was in the hospice house. We were all there, spending his last hours on earth reading his favorite Bible verses, telling stories, whispering in his ear so he knew he was never alone. When the afternoon came to a close, right before the nurses' shift change, one of the nurses came into the room. She leaned over his bed and said something so touching and personal, I'll never forget it: "If I don't see you tomorrow, I just want to thank you for your service to our country." I think we all prayed silently that those thoughtful words made their way into Bop's consciousness.

His last breaths were separated by long pauses, and the room changed as we all gathered around his bed, knowing the end was near. My sister-in-law was there with her eight-month-old twins, who were at that effervescent stage of constant baby babble. But even the twins were calm and quiet for a full fifteen minutes that felt both very hard and very holy. This was a sacrament I had never before experienced: the sacrament of dying.

If you've ever attended the death of someone you loved, you might have experienced a sort of ethereal moment when a hush falls over the room. It's the kind of quiet that comes right when a spring thunderstorm ends, with amber light pooling into the room, making long shadows. In the quiet, you have a sense of this person you love slipping out of his skin and walking away with someone you can't see but can almost feel. It sounds spooky, but as I've pondered my own departure from this incredible earth, it's a most reassuring thing.

Then Bop was gone, and the twins started fussing again.

During the days immediately following his death, I worried about whether we'd adequately prepared our daughters for Bop's death. I worried we cried too much or too little; that we talked too much about dying or not quite enough. That I didn't answer their questions about my own tears as directly as I should have.

I worried that I relied too much on metaphors about doorways and tulips to do the hard work of telling the children, in frank terms, that Bop was dying.

But then spring came again, with its perennial hope floating on the breeze. And I remembered what the tulips knew.

There is a season for everything—the hard things and the beautiful things, the living things and the dying things, the things that grow fast and the Ancient Way where things grow slow.

The tulips never doubted spring would come. They bloomed, lifting their faces toward heaven. And our daughters, they plucked petals right off the plants, and I didn't scold them even a little.

I did what they asked me to do next. Those two girls said, "Drive to the cemetery," and I did just that.

I drove them up the hill, to the Lee family burial plots—where Paul, Milo, and Ole now rest—and I knelt down beside the girls as they spread the soft petals on Bop's grave.

No Spring Skips Its Turn

You can't keep winter from coming, but you can't keep spring from coming, either. You'll want to remember that truth in the winters of life—in the hospitals, in counselors' offices, at gravesides, when you're reading the text message wherein he tells you it's over or the email informing you they gave your dream job to someone else.

Nothing—*nothing*—can keep spring from coming again. Like the great outdoorsman Hal Borland said, "No winter lasts forever; no spring skips its turn."

Spring is a fulfilled promise, and even though you don't ever forget winter existed, there's a warmth that bursts forth within you when those first flowers bloom and when familiar birds you haven't heard in ages start singing in the ash trees. You wake up one morning and, still in your pajamas, you open the front door and say to yourself, "This—*this!*—is a beautiful spring day!"

You turn off the furnace and you open the bedroom windows and you thumb through the gardening book you bought the year before. You take a walk and you leave your jacket at home and you feel the urge to plant once more.

I will not race through the strange sadness that spring sometimes brings—like the aching absence of a devoted farmer who died too soon. Yet I know this season gives us not only Good Friday but Resurrection Sunday.

I am learning to set aside expectations, but I will not let go of hope.

I will ask God to give me the courage to enter into each day with open hands, for this is the gesture of letting go.

I will open my hands to let go of control.

Let go of my plans.

Let go of my preferences.

Let go of my expectations.

That doesn't mean I'm giving up. It means I'm giving in to the will of the One who made me.

God never fails. He just doesn't. He is a promise keeper and the holder of the plan. He is working miles ahead of us, putting pieces of this great big puzzle together. The Ancient Way of Growing Slow says the puzzle has dark and light pieces, some smooth and some jagged on the edges. On my journey down the Ancient Way, there will be a time to weep, and a time to laugh.

A time for expectations to be unfulfilled, and a time for expectations to be exceeded far more than we would have dreamed.

A time to mourn, and a time to dance.

He is making everything beautiful in its time.

And when he does, I will dance.

REMEMBER

An unexpected life is not
the same as a bad life.

REFLECT

What's your favorite season of the year?

....

....

....

Think about the literal and metaphorical spring seasons
of your life. Does spring feel like a do-over or a season of
dashed hopes?

....

....

....

In what ways do expectations get in the way of your
relationship with God?

....

....

Are you standing at the crossroads of your will and
God's will? Imagine yourself opening up your hands, your
heart, and your will to the Lord.

....

....

....

RETURN

At the end of each chapter, we return to the soil.

Even in the last months of his life, my father-in-law had a desire to keep planting and keep sowing. He wanted to work the fields with his son for that last harvest of his life.

As you think about what you're planting now, what harvest is most important to you? Perhaps you're considering the fruit of your daily work or the goals you set for yourself at the beginning of the year. Perhaps you are pondering seeds you've planted into the people around you. Knowing the answer to this question will help you on your own Growing Slow journey, because it will inform your priorities and how you spend your days on earth, where time goes much faster than we ever imagined it would. Make a list of those priorities here.

CHAPTER 6

YOU ARE NOT FALLING BEHIND

Ironically, the strongest pressure to "grow fast," instead of slow, came during the years when I started writing books about Jesus. I say this is ironic, because nothing Jesus ever said communicated an ethic of "grow fast."

Let me explain how it happened for me. This isn't something we authors talk much about publicly, but there's an expectation of growth in the publishing industry. Growth in sales. Growth in influence. Growth in something called "platform," which is essentially an indication of how many people follow you on social media. If you have a decent-sized platform, it signals to the publisher that you have a built-in audience who already likes what you have to say. This is not a criticism of the publishing industry. Publishing houses have to pay to keep the lights on, and they can't take on everybody who wants to write a book.

At the time when my publishing career took off, I was considered a "small-platform author." I knew what a blessing it was to get a book contract. Sometimes I thought I had snuck in the back door of the publishing house when no one was looking. (There's a name for this: imposter syndrome. It's usually accompanied by an author curling into a fetal position and rocking back and forth in the corner during the final stages of writing. Yes, I was a ball of positivity while composing the paragraphs that became this book.)

As my publishing career took off, internal pressure mounted. I knew that if my first book didn't sell well, there would be no chance of getting another book published.

Growing Slow didn't feel like an option.

The Enneagram 3 performer in me was up for the challenge. There were social media platforms to learn. New ways to connect with readers. New audiences to reach in states where I'd never set foot before. It felt exciting for a while, but there were nights when I stretched out on my hotel room bed in some never-before-visited state with the drapes closed, when I felt gutted, hollowed out.

Meanwhile, as months turned to years, I watched new influencers and entrepreneurs hop onto the scene. In just a few months, it seemed, they were mastering the same platforms I'd been feeding with daily content for years. Twenty-somethings with perfect skin, hair extensions, and a branded look danced across arena stages in Converse. Their fast growth was being rewarded.

And here I was . . . *Growing Slow.*

The urge to run faster and work harder was undeniable. Yet a question began to emerge: *Do I really want a fast life that rubs me raw?*

I had to ask myself, *In the rush to become a "somebody," have I forgotten that I already am?*

Slow change began. And I emphasize the word *slow* here. It began in hotel rooms, with late nights of scrambling to schedule the next day's social media posts. With the readjustment of work priorities. With the stripping of my schedule. And finally, with the visit to the doctor who told me my physical problems were the result of a hurried heart.

All systems pointed to one conclusion: *Growing Slow was no longer an option but a necessity.*

This new and strange slowness coincided with the slow growth on our farm. That whole rainy spring, everything felt behind, not quite what it should be, because the wet fields prevented planting.

One day, on one of my prayer drives, I found myself on the skinny dirt road that borders the back 80. I pulled over to the side of the road, rolled down my window, and snapped a photo of the wet and crop-less field. A bank of clouds inched across the horizon. In that moment, something important hit me. I have so often felt the way that field looked: with no growth evident because planting was running behind. At key points in my life, I've felt behind—behind in my career, in my life trajectory, and, as a late bloomer in faith, even in my spirituality.

That awareness shifted something in me. My fear of falling behind had been a reason for my rushed existence. It's why I felt like I had to be so insanely productive all the time, as if life is a constant game of catch-up. Even my calendar made me feel behind, with all those little squares waiting for neat Xs. Hop on Instagram for about two seconds, and you can get this weird sense of who's ahead of you—and how far you need to go.

If life is a marathon, many of us are comparing our first mile to someone else's twenty-sixth. Our hearts and bodies suffer self-inflicted wounds when we do this.

Our culture will make you think there are milestones. But there aren't. You aren't a cornfield. You are a person. You aren't a corn seed. You are a soul. The growth in you isn't dependent on weather or the right kind of fertilizer. Your progress can't be predicted by the *Old Farmer's Almanac*.

Here's the thing nobody talks about when it comes to your pace of growth: There are no set milestones. Not for when you get married. Not for when you have kids—or even *if* you have them. Not for when you earn a certain salary or master a certain set of tasks. There just aren't milestones for any of these things.

Sometimes, you look around at everyone else's progress and feel like you're a failure.

Their dreams are coming true.

Their kids are making the honor roll.

Their marriages are fruitful and fun.

Their businesses are thriving.

Meanwhile, you've just got a pocketful of unfulfilled dreams that leave you dissatisfied. You have setbacks and little fruit to show for your hard work. You feel weak, like you're failing. Deep inside, you wonder if you're disappointing God.

Friend, you are not failing, I promise you.

Is weakness all you've got right now? God can work with weakness. Scripture says that's the place where the Spirit steps in to help us.[1]

Do you feel like giving up, even though you know God has called you to this task? If that's you, chin up, friend. Be steadfast and immovable, "knowing that in the Lord your labor is not in vain."[2]

If you saw your progress the way God does, you'd never doubt for a moment that you're making a difference.

We don't need more memes or motivational speakers to sell us a new way to move ahead. *We need permission to be where we are.*

Did you know you are allowed to walk at your own pace? You are allowed to shut down the computer at five o'clock. You are allowed to take the time you need to figure things out. There's no such thing as an overnight success, and your life will not be ruined if you stick to your steady pace.

In the race between the tortoise and the hare, remember who won.

Look around you: there is growth in your fields, inching heavenward, not with brute force, but by the will of the Divine Farmer who makes all things beautiful in their time. A corn plant never compares itself to the one beside it. It never fights the clock or doubts the harvest will come. In that back 80, Scott eventually planted millions of corn seeds, each one no bigger than a fingernail. Weeks later than was typical, the first leaf emerged, followed by a second, then a third. In time, each plant was tasseled and silked and did all the other miraculous things a corn plant does until it reaches full maturity.

At the right time we will harvest a good crop if we don't give up, or quit.[3]

The harvest is coming. In its time. You are not falling behind.

You Don't Get to Know the Time

Growing Slow is about living at peace with God's timing. There's a story about his timing that rests like an anchor in the first chapter of Acts. In the story, the resurrected Jesus presents himself bodily to his followers. He offers instructions, then ascends to heaven. Imagine yourself as one of those eager followers. Imagine how intently you would listen, hanging on every word and wanting to do exactly what the Savior asked you to do.

The one question these followers asked is essentially this: "When?"[4]

When will your plan come to pass, Jesus?
Isn't this the question we're all asking? When, Lord, when?
When will I see the growth?
When is it my time?
When will I get the "lucky break"?
When will I get the promotion?
When will God's promises unfold for me?
When will my dream come true?

Jesus' answer to his followers in Acts is his answer to us today:

> "You don't get to know the time. Timing is the Father's busi-
> ness. What you'll get is the Holy Spirit. And when the Holy
> Spirit comes on you, you will be able to be my witnesses . . .
> even to the ends of the world."[5]

Then Jesus disappeared, and all of his followers stood around, looking at an empty sky.

I know what it feels like to stand under a wide-open sky and wonder if God's promises will unfold—or if I even heard him correctly. We all ask it: *When is it my turn?*

Jesus answers clearly, "You don't get to know the time. Timing is the Father's business."

This is what I know for sure: If God put those seeds in your hands, and if he put that field before you, he will let you know when. Keep taking the next step. Tend to the things you know produce fruit: prayer, surrounding yourself with healthy people, sleep, moments of stillness, your wellness and wholeness and well-being.

Meanwhile, don't assume nothing is growing. While you are planting seeds, *he* is growing *you*. Let's not forget that we are fields, not just farmers. Deep spiritual growth is happening under the surface.

A seedling will burst forth.

In his will. In his way. In his timing.

Everyday Miracles

As spring comes to a close, I'm on the gravel road again, the one where we began our spring together.

Not long ago, this field was a soggy mess. Then the sun came, not as hot and plentiful as we wanted, but it came. It's warm enough that I can roll down the windows. The warmth feels like a resurrection.

From my vantage point on this gravel road, this is not a view of an ideal field with ideal growth.

But look closely; the crops are growing. Revisit what Jesus said: "A man scatters seed on the ground. Night and day, whether he sleeps or gets up, the seed sprouts and grows, *though he does not know how.*"[6]

There is great relief in these words. God didn't check in with us on how to make a seed push against the dirt with Herculean strength. He didn't ask us how to make the clouds produce rain or how to make the sun rise once more.

It happens simply because God made it so.

This is a miracle, isn't it? A Growing Slow miracle.

Some people say the word *miracle* should be reserved for big things, like surviving a near-death experience. Einstein is credited with saying, "There are only two ways to live your life. One is as though nothing is a miracle. The other is as though everything is a miracle."

I choose to call any growth a miracle.

As you consider your fields, may our farm be an encouragement to you to keep planting. I imagine you now, standing in faith at the edge of your field, looking for proof that growth will appear. Keep looking. Keep believing. Growth will come. The field in front of you and the seeds cupped in your hands were intended for you, by God's design.

God isn't just hanging out with the people killin' it today. He isn't spending his whole day applauding all the people getting their crap together with some new organizational system or exercise program. He is with *you* in this slow and sometimes imperceptible growth.

And when you do see growth, take a moment to say a prayer of thanks. Hold the moment close to your heart so that you won't forget the gentle bursting forth of an everyday miracle.

REMEMBER

If you saw your progress the way that
God does, you'd never doubt for a
moment that you're making a difference.

REFLECT

Do you feel behind in this season of your life? If so, in
what ways?

....

....

....

What cultural expectations make you feel like you're
falling behind? For example, when you should be
engaged, married, have kids, earn a certain salary, master
a certain skill.

....

....

....

....

As you pursue your dreams, where has God's timing
seemed off? What comfort, if any, does the story from
Acts 1:1–12 bring you?

....

....

....

RETURN

At the end of each chapter, we return to the soil.

Take a moment to call out the small growth you see emerging in the fields you've planted, perhaps from seeds you planted long ago. Start a running list. Here are a few of mine:

> My daughters, now teens, are daily praying Scripture over themselves.
>
> Trust with a friend, built over the years, means she is willing to share her heart with me as she bears the burden of cancer.
>
> I have successfully developed the habit of exercising on a regular basis and feel stronger than ever.

Add yours below.

....

....

....

....

....

....

....

....

....

....

....

PART 2

SUMMER GROWTH

The farmer waits for the precious crop
from the earth, being patient with it until it
receives the early and the late rains. You also
must be patient. Strengthen your hearts, for
the coming of the Lord is near.

JAMES 5:7–8 NRSV

CHAPTER 7

BUILT TO LAST

The romantic in me loves autumn. The melancholic in me needs a little bit of winter. The optimist in me thrives with the hopefulness of spring.

But the child in me needs summer.

Summer, oh summer.

Summer is a dip in the deep end of a pool and the smell of fresh-cut grass on the lawn. It's the elated cry of *School's out!* as kids stream out of the building and pile into yellow buses for the last time until fall. Summer is fireflies in the air, kittens in the barn, and hamburgers on the charcoal grill. We'll serve those burgers on skillet-toasted buns, alongside sliced tomatoes and Iowa sweet corn slathered in real butter.

For farmers, there's still work to be done in summer—they need to keep a keen eye on things like pests and weeds and weather. Animals need feeding; fences need mending.

But on our farm, summers offer brief respites when we can get away.

When the girls were quite young, we started saving up money for summer road trips. We didn't want to wait until "someday" to make memories together, out in this great big wonderful world with its breathtaking mountain vistas, bubbling trout streams, and expansive cities of tall, mirrored buildings.

Of course, traveling with little humans was intensely chaotic. There's nothing quite like a road trip to test the limits of a family's love. Someone always needs to pee when you're miles away from a bathroom. Someone is always blaming someone else for farting, chewing too loudly, or crossing over the iconic invisible line that has, for generations, existed to keep one kid from invading another kid's personal space. Thanks to the Tetris skills my husband and I honed in high school, we could arrange the trunk with all the required equipment we needed in the early days: breast pump, portable crib, diapers, strollers, DVDs, gallons of hand sanitizer, an unreasonable number of "must-have" blankies, and the children's weight in Goldfish crackers. Once, before we set out on an adventure, our young Anna secretly emptied her suitcase of all of its contents and replaced it entirely with stuffed animals. We didn't realize what she'd done until we arrived at the hotel late at night. She was without a toothbrush or clean underwear, but hey, she had enough plush critters to fill a small ark.

Even with the chaos, we insisted on traveling each summer, partly to learn about the world, and partly to learn about ourselves.

Travel is mercifully easier with teens who own AirPods. The girls are (mostly) kind to one another, mind the invisible line, and even help plan the itinerary. When I look at my girls, I see summer personified, growing brighter as days lengthen and carrying a warm light and curiosity within them. I never thought I'd enjoy parenting teens—I harbored mild trepidation that this would be an angst-filled season—but spending time with them is one of my greatest joys.

Our summer trips have occasionally taken us far from home. In mid-June, after the corn and soybeans had been planted, we caught a flight across the ocean. Our family spent two weeks touring London, Bath, and Paris, staying in Airbnbs and stopping at vendor stands for cheese, crepes, cappuccinos, and crusty bread wrapped in paper.

While walking the cobblestone streets of Bath, Lydia carried with her a backpack of books, and at points in the journey—the Royal Crescent, the Pump Room, the Theatre Royal—she would produce a Jane Austen novel and perform for us a short reading, accompanied by grand flourishes and a terrible British accent. The theatrics annoyed her younger sister to no end.

While we each had varying interest in Jane Austen, we could all agree on the impressiveness of Europe's palaces and cathedrals. I don't think you have to build a big cathedral to impress God, but there's something very breathtaking about a structure like that—one that rises high to scrape the sky, amplifying the voices of centuries of dreamers and grievers and saints and schemers and vagabonds and anyone who accidentally encountered something holy when they thought they might simply "get a nice photo" of a building.

All around us, permanence and legacy made itself evident. Everything was, as they say, "built to last"—not just in those grand structures like Westminster Abbey, the Royal Crescent, or the Arc de Triomphe, but in tucked-away places like old hotels and centuries-old taverns.

One afternoon, while walking in London, we stumbled upon a bookstore called Hatchards. We marveled at the five-story building with its impressive wooden staircase. A saleswoman helped Lydia peruse the Jane Austen section and later told us that the shop had been selling books since 1797. Think about that for a moment. The creaky floorboards of that building have supported the written word for something like eight generations.

"Built to last." Those were the words Scott kept repeating as we walked around the city.

After we returned home, I asked myself, *What does it take to grow something that's built to last?*

For Hatchards, longevity is credited to a great location, a charming facility, a dedicated and knowledgeable staff—and the mad audacity to keep pushing forward no matter what. I want that kind of mad audacity reflected in my own life.

In a throwaway culture driven by consumerism, Hatchards stands out. The store is an exception in a world that seems to favor excessive, single-use production. Instead of repairing, we replace. We don't patch things; we purge.

Washing machines last—what?—ten years?

Some of what we buy is actually built to fail. It sounds crazy, but it's true. There's even a term for it: "planned obsolescence."

Planned obsolescence is a business strategy where products are designed to deliberately fail. They cannot be repaired, require updates, or have a set lifespan.[1] If you've had to go to the store for an update on your mobile phone, you have experienced planned obsolescence. Not only do you eventually buy an upgraded phone, you have to purchase a new charger or adapter to go with it. The entire fashion industry is built around what's in style—a form of planned obsolescence where you're convinced that the clothes in your closet are outdated.

It's not a stretch to say that this mindset infects what we care about most: relationships, faith communities, our health, even the land. We all want new and beautiful things to spring forth to new life. We want our lives to reflect meaningful work that can change the world. But growth that stands the test of time simply cannot be rushed.

We can't expect to have Hatchards longevity while running at a Hardee's pace.

Yet we are running at warp speed with an insatiable hunger for immediate results.

People want meaning and connection, but they don't always take time to build the foundation that will help make a relationship last.

A couple starts attending a new church, but even a little dissatisfaction can send them out the door in search of something better somewhere else.

We eat so fast, we don't taste our food.

We rarely take the long way home, missing the scenery, because we want to get where we want to go, and we want to get there now.

Hurry is the enemy of beauty.

Beauty comes when we stay instead of run; when we taste instead of shovel in; when we take the long way home after work and see the brightest blue sky open before us.

Quicker is not always better.

There's nothing wrong with meeting goals swiftly. Some moments really are made for hustling. But the desire to build quickly is dangerous. It can hurt the foundational pillars that hold up our relationships, businesses, and health.

Let's stop glorifying the end results and start embracing the day-by-day process of building something beautiful with our lives. We have bought into the deception that a meaningful life is the result of achieving goals, but meaning isn't found in the rush for results. Quite often, meaning is found in the struggle.

With all that is within me, I am convinced that God is far less concerned with how quickly we meet quotas and more interested in the people we are becoming as we embrace slow growth. He takes joy in seeing how we are willing to walk in obedience while refusing to compromise our personal integrity in the name of achievement. God delights in watching us grow the virtues of patience and perseverance in our lives. It brings him happiness to see us grow into the kind of women who hold ourselves to high ideals, who develop habits of fidelity and humility, who lean on him in the struggle, who sacrifice, who trust that he will keep his promises even when we can't see progress.

Slow growth is less fixated on the end prize and more about

long-term personal transformation. God is making each of us built to last—like Hatchards with skin on, with souls and hearts that beat like this: *Jesus, Jesus, Jesus.*

Remember, in chapter 3, where we learned anew that each of us is God's field? There's more:

> You are God's field. You are also God's building.[2]

Brick by brick, God is building you into the fullness of all he created you to be as a daughter of God. God's ways of maturing his people can seem needlessly—even painfully—slow. But God is not slow in the way that we think of slowness.

> The Lord is not slow in keeping his promise, as some understand slowness. Instead he is patient with you.[3]

There is no ten-step plan to become a better you. It's a plan with a million steps, taken incrementally over a life, toward a glorious harvest. When you lay your head down on your pillow at night, you may wonder what you have to show for your day. If that's you, I wish you could see what God sees! You are building something with your life, something built to last.

The story of Hatchards reveals that it's possible to build something that lasts, something that will outlive us. It's possible to live a small, quiet life, and make a mark on our world, simply by taking care of our people and our fields—in the same way generations of Hatchards' owners and employees have taken care of a store since 1797.

What do you want to last?

What will matter most five years from now? Ten years from now? One hundred years from now?

Maybe you want to leave a trail of love and kindness. Maybe

you want to be known as generous, or wise, or the kind of person who gave everyone a reason to laugh and smile.

As for me, I hope my marriage is built to last, a steady foundation and an example for generations to come. I hope my books are built to last, offering timeless encouragement to real souls for years to come. I hope my parenting is built to last—that I'm living life in a way that helps my children and their children love Jesus with everything that is in them.

My church. My community. My faith. My friendships. I pray it's all built to last. Let's refuse to bend to impulse, instead doing our little part every day to help create goodness and beauty that will stand the test of time.

The more I ponder these questions of legacy, the more I come alive. Because I don't feel the pressure to make something marvelous. I am seeing, instead, how God is making something marvelous in me—a soul built to love him and enjoy him forever.

The truth is, in one hundred years, I likely won't be remembered at all. My books will be out of print. Who knows if my little church will still be standing? Perhaps my name will be written by my great-great-grandson on an ancestral chart his teacher sends home for a school project. But God will have built something to last in me. Every struggle, every heartbreak, every success, every failure, teaches me something about who God is. He is dropping seeds into the soil of my heart.

I hope these words bring you encouragement today. Even if your family doesn't remember your name one hundred years from now, something is growing in you, and through you.

Who you are becoming today influences the "becoming" of those closest to you right now. And their "becoming" influences the "becoming" of real souls in the next generation and in untold generations after that. It's a ripple effect that spans across generations—"That a people not yet created may praise the LORD."[4]

Built to Fall

A few months ago, our family took another trip, this time to a beach far from home. One sunny day, from under the shade of my umbrella, I watched as a father and son spent hours building a sandcastle. I'd look up from my book every now and then to see a girl or an old man or another dad stop for a few minutes to help. It was a pretty cool picture of community—all these strangers under one big sky, taking time to work together simply for the sake of making something beautiful. By the end of the day, the castle had multiple towers, a moat, and features like molded stone facing and stairs, all painstakingly sculpted into the sand. The father and his boy stood back and admired their work. They had built their castle far enough from the ocean's edge to avoid the incoming tide. Still, there was little doubt that—despite the many hours of work that went into the structure and all the hands that built it—the castle was eventually going down.

The next morning, our family headed to the same spot on the beach. We found chairs and spread out our towels on them. I looked around to find the castle, and predictably, it was in ruins.

But behind the ruins were the man and the son who built it, and they were building once again. To me, it all seemed rather pointless, to begin rebuilding something that surely wouldn't stand. I walked over to talk to them.

"So sorry about your castle, guys," I said. "I really enjoyed watching you build it yesterday."

The father spoke with a smile. "Oh, don't be sorry. Not at all. We know these castles won't last," he said as he patted a handful of sand into a new turret. I watched his son, who was happily hauling a bucket of wet sand to the opposite end of the new castle. The boy seemed as carefree as his dad, who, as it turned out, was an architect by trade.

I asked the dad what had happened to the castle. It wasn't the tide that swept it away. It wasn't the beach-combing equipment either. Rather, a group of children had jumped on top of the structure, and it crumbled under their weight.

I would have been so ticked. But that father was unruffled. "We come to this beach for a week every year, and our favorite part is building castles," he said. "They never last. But this is what we do. It's hard work, but mostly, it's just a lot of fun."

I thanked them again and went back to my chair. The dedication of that dad and his son shifted something in me. They built for the sake of building. They did it for fun, for the enjoyment of the process, for the opportunity to work side by side. Sure, they stood back at the end of each day and admired what they had made together. But the end product was not the purpose. The purpose was in the process.

You may very well grow some pretty amazing Hatchard-esque things in this life—slowly and sustainably, as God intended. Those things may last a very long time, indeed.

But not everything you build is meant to last. Not everything will produce a measurable legacy. Your best efforts may be washed away, trampled, or run over. Your best work may one day be forgotten. No one but God may know about the most meaningful things you did with your life because they were done in obscurity, when no one was watching but him.

You might think that what you've built with your life so far isn't all that grand. But maybe that's not the point, anyway. It's not what you're building; it's *who* you are building *with*.

Come to the shore. Kneel next to your Father, and get your knees dirty as the sun warms your back. And when the day comes to a close, stand up next to your Father, and take a moment to admire what you've done together. Then, watch as he turns to you, squeezes your hand, and says, "Wasn't that fun? Let's do it again tomorrow."

REMEMBER

Let's stop glorifying the end results,
and start embracing the day-by-
day process of building something
beautiful with our lives.

REFLECT

On page 76, I talk about planned obsolescence. How have
you seen this at work in our culture or in your life?

....

....

....

How does our culture make it hard for us to accept
the kind of foundational growth that keeps a place like
Hatchards standing for more than two centuries?

....

....

....

....

When you reflect on your life, do you sense that what
you are building is more like Hatchards, more like a
sandcastle, or some of both?

....

....

....

....

What precious benefits come from building slowly? Consider the question as it relates to your relationships, your work, and your legacy.

....

....

....

....

RETURN

At the end of each chapter, we
return to the soil. Today, though,
let's return to the sand.

Imagine yourself working alongside your Father, building something beautiful. Imagine his hand brushing up against yours. Imagine what it would be like to value these precious moments of building alongside your Father, not to build castles or kingdoms, but simply to experience his love. He's building something *in you*. Can you sense it? Write down one area of your life where you need God to transform you.

....

....

....

....

....

....

....

CHAPTER 8

THE LITTLE THINGS ARE THE BIG THINGS

The words popped into my inbox at precisely the right time, on a day when I was feeling discouraged:

"Jennifer, I am writing to let you know that God delights in you."

There were other remarks, but the part about God delighting in me was the part I clung to. "God delights in you." Could there be any more beautiful words?

The note was from Dave, a pastor who lived about a half hour from our farm. Over the years, he had become a dear friend to my husband and me. Dave wasn't our pastor, but he was a spiritual mentor. Quite regularly, he would drop me a line, reminding me that I was loved by God just as I was, not as I thought I should be. Dave had a Brennan Manning-esque quality to him that helped you see that no matter how badly you'd blown it, God would not walk out on you. Dave seemed to have a sixth sense of when I had pushed myself into burnout and overwhelm, and he always stepped in at just the right time to encourage me. He mostly just made me feel loved by God. He ended all of his notes with those four words: "God delights in you."

Dave had a ministry of words, and I wasn't the only one on the receiving end. He spread kindness everywhere he went, like confetti. If you were his friend on Facebook, there was a pretty solid chance you'd get a birthday greeting on your Facebook wall, a reminder that "God delights in you."

Lately, I've reflected a lot on Dave's pattern of encouragement, and two things stick out to me. First, of course, was his steady reminder of where we stand with God. We can put away all external expectation, the desire to achieve, the pressure to be more. When we do that, we can see clearly how God's delight is simply in us as people, not as machines of productivity. God doesn't delight in our output as much as he delights simply in our ordinary, busted-up selves. On the days when we feel unseen, unappreciated, or under-valued, we never have to guess how Jesus feels about us. In those seasons when life seems like an unending chain of chores, bills, and monotony, I need to remember that God delights in me. Here I am: seen, wholly loved, fully valued. That's the first thing that sticks with me.

The second thing that stuck with me is the lesson on constant repeat in Dave's life: The little things are the big things, and those are the things that will change the world. A few years ago, following a long illness, Dave died. For weeks after he passed away, many of his friends wrote lengthy tributes to Dave on their Facebook walls. They recalled the miles of kind words Dave used to pave a road that led people straight to Jesus. You see, Dave did a lot of important things in his life, in his first career at a radio station, and then later, as a pastor of numerous congregations. But no one talked about Dave's resume after he died. They talked about his kindness and his words.

Let's not miss this. We think it's the big things that are going to change the world, but it's all the little things, added together, that make life matter and give it meaning. I believe this with all my heart.

Behold your fields. Take a moment to inventory what you're

growing. Don't make the mistake of disregarding those tiny shoots of green as forgettable. Friend, those are the things that no one else could grow but you—the unrepeatable sequence of DNA that makes you *you*!

Don't dismiss the gift of small and slow.

Your small, slow progress is still progress.

Your small, slow-growth church is still a church.

Your small, slow faith is still faith.

Your small, slow start is still a start.

I have had to fight against the temptation to dismiss the little things. When our girls were young, I often wondered whether what I was doing meant anything at all. I had moved from a successful career in the news business to this life as an accidental farm girl. In those first years, I had very few friends, two young children, a husband who was suddenly a farmer, and insecurities about my inability to do all things farm-wifey. Life was a series of nighttime wake-ups, unending nursing sessions, picture books read and reread, and applesauce scooped onto Dora the Explorer lunch plates.

It is often said that, for moms, the days are long, but the years are short. How true this is. Our girls are teens, and as I write this, one is a year away from starting college. In hindsight, I have begun to see what mattered most. Every touch, every gentle word, every morning prayer, every tuck-in, every silly text, every meal, every late-night harmonizing session around the piano—every single little thing mattered.

I know the little things mattered because I have begun to see fruit emerge from all those seeds planted in the middle of long nights, long car rides, long days of monotony on the floor of a playroom, or the floor of a bathroom when they were ill.

I am not saying I have been the perfect mom, nor am I saying my children are perfect, but I am saying that learning to be steadfast in the little things made a difference.

Looking back, I remember all the times I wished I could coordinate their nap schedules so I could get "real work" accomplished, work that was measurable and noticeable. I wish I could have had a crystal ball to see how my faithfulness in the little moments would matter so much years later.

My girls have a deep sense of justice, of right and wrong, of serving, of standing up for the underdog, of the importance of bringing Christ's light into the world. I want to reiterate that our children are not perfect. There have been weeds in these fields. But there are moments I never want to forget, too. Even in our daughters' darkest hours as teenagers, they have held fast to the hand of God, believing he would bring purpose from their pain, even if they had to wait all the way to heaven to know what it is. Anna is still in the midst of her emotional healing, but just this morning showed me a verse she has been clinging to: "What no eye has seen, nor ear heard, nor the heart of man imagined, what God has prepared for those who love him."[1] She says the verse reminds her that God has great plans for her.

We all want to know we matter, and that the seeds we are planting will bear fruit, but that fruit might look different than we first dreamed.

Just recently, I was asked to serve as a spiritual director for a weekend-long Christian teen retreat. Both of my daughters have been a part of this particular ministry, so I asked Anna what the role of the spiritual director was. I thought she would give me a list of duties: leading prayer sessions, giving talks, and so on. But instead, she said:

"Your main job is to give a lot of hugs."

Of all of the things that the previous retreat's spiritual director—herself a mom of teens—had done, the love she expressed through hugs was what stood out most. Anna had come away from that retreat feeling intensely loved by Jesus, and now it was clear that one of the ways he made his presence known that weekend was through the repeated kindness of a mom who gave away countless hugs.

We undervalue the little things, but let me say it once more for the people in the back: the little things are the big things, and these are the things that change the world.

So many people I know minimize themselves with the phrase "just a."

"I'm just a mom."

"I'm just a janitor."

"I'm just a _____."

That phrase—"just a"—needs to be stricken from our vocabulary. "Just a" feeds into the belief that we aren't doing enough with our lives to give them meaning.

The weekend I worked at that teen spiritual retreat, one of my friends spoke at a national conference in front of thousands of women. But I refuse to say that my work is less important than hers, or that I am "just a spiritual director" charged with the unofficial task of giving hugs.

There are times when I am called to stages, but hear me now: you don't have to hold a microphone to do something big for Jesus. Before I am up on those stages, I say a prayer for all the people who make it possible for me to communicate the good news—the tech person who makes sure my voice is projected, the administrative assistant who printed off the handouts, and the janitor who swept the stage before I ever set foot on it.

Most of my life is not onstage. Most of it is unfolding on a farm, in unseen places that will never make headlines. And those are the things that have made me the kind of person I want to be: someone who connects with others and—I pray—blesses them a little bit along the way. Someone who shows up at the Porter Funeral Home to hug a grieving widow. Someone who says yes when Trish recruits a bunch of us to roam the town streets on a cold December night, singing Christmas carols for anyone within earshot. And on that Christmas caroling evening, when we stop at the doorway of an elderly woman, and she comes out in her nightgown, leaning over her walker and dabbing at tears with her hankie while we sing at her doorway—well, I want to be someone who cries right along with her.

I want to be someone who isn't in such a hurry that I forget to care in little ways that have lasting value.

Say it with me one more time: *The little things are the big things*.

Our Maker values the small things: the loaf, the cup, the mustard seed, the quiet prayer whispered into the dark.

I see you there, in your field, watching all that goodness bloom. I know how tempted you might be to discount your bits of growth as a bunch of little "justs."

But friend, you didn't "just" put dinner on the table last night.

You didn't "just" drive your friend to chemo today.

You didn't "just" send the sympathy card to the grieving widow.

You didn't "just" go to the trouble of letting everyone know that God delights in them. Someone a lot like you did that.

When we exit earth for heaven, we might not have a lot of money or big ministries or pretty things to leave behind for the people we love. But we can be rich in small acts of faithfulness, born of kindness and our love for Jesus. We can leave an inheritance of love.

It matters.

Your faithfulness matters. Your kind words matter. Your choice to follow Jesus matters.

Just you wait and see.

I really don't think we are going to show up in heaven just to have the Lord say to us, "You had a pretty impressive Instagram feed," or "Great job hitting that record-breaking sales goal that one time."

I think he mostly just wants to give you a hug, hold you tight, and whisper in your ear, "I delight in you!"

REMEMBER

The little things are the big things.
And the little things are the things
that will change the world.

REFLECT

Where in your life do you feel unseen or unvalidated?

....

....

....

How does comparison tend to minimize the little things
we are growing?

....

....

....

Think of a time in your life when you invested in a "little
thing" and can now, in hindsight, see its significance.
To get your thoughts flowing, consider your prayers,
kindnesses that seemed insignificant at the time, and
acts of service.

....

....

....

....

How can you validate the small things growing in the life of someone else who might feel unseen? Reach out to them today.

....

....

....

RETURN

At the end of each chapter, we return to the soil.

Consider seeds you've planted in the small things of life—perhaps your small group of friends, your small ministry, your little text messages of encouragement, which you might discount as meaningless. Take a moment to appreciate the fact that these little things have the potential to make a tremendous difference in your circle of influence. What are some ways you have made this kind of difference in the lives of those around you?

....

....

....

....

....

....

....

....

....

....

CHAPTER 9

WHAT IT ALL COMES DOWN TO

The reason we do more, push a little harder, move a bit faster, and run around like a crazy person all comes down to this in the end: we want love.

We try to get love in a million ways. For me, it's been performance and achievement. For you, maybe it's the same. Or maybe it's sex, food, excessive exercise, distracting consumption of media, shopping, attempts to please your parents. Even something that looks completely selfless, like serving others, can be a way to get someone to love you back.

But our good grades can't love us back. Our moisturized skin can't love us back. Our food rules can't love us back. Our achievements can't love us back. Our perfectly good works can't love us back. Our hurry-up, hurry-up approach to life can't love us back.

We know there's nothing we can do to lose God's love, right? Well, there's nothing we can do to earn it, either.

For it is by grace you have been saved, through faith—and
this is not from yourselves, it is the gift of God—not by works,
so that no one can boast.[1]

So why do we make it more than that? We've heard the ser-
mons, taken the Bible studies, underlined the verses, and still we try
to make everything far more complicated than it should be.

I mean, here is this incredible gift that God holds out to us, yet
we insist on settling for second-rate substitutes, like approval or a
bit of fame.

It starts when we are young.

When I was a kid, I was obsessed with being liked, which
shaped my earliest ambitions. My worldview was quite small, so I
thought being liked mostly had to do with how good you were on the
basketball court, or if the boys thought you were cute. My obsession
with my hair and resulting overuse of Aqua Net hairspray are now
to blame for a huge hole in the ozone layer.

Most days, I felt like I was on the outside looking in. So many
of my memories are of being left out or relentlessly teased.

Moments in high school lunchrooms have a weird way of scar-
ring you.

As an adult, I tend to be an avoider. It's a carryover technique
I learned early on: withdraw when you are struggling. People may
sense there's something wrong, but I am reluctant to share how I
feel deep down. Beginning in my childhood, withdrawing was a
technique I used to insulate myself from pain. There was a lot of
shame that came with being a teased kid, who was easily prone to
tears and criticized for being "too sensitive." I remember thinking
that was the way it would always be. I'd never be good enough,
never be truly accepted, never be on the inside, so I had to figure
out how to cope. This will probably come as a shock to my high
school classmates, because I had carefully curated my image, and

most of them probably thought I had my life together. But I was a hot mess just waiting for the school bell to ring.

When I was alone, I experienced moments of quiet desperation. I never had a plan to take my own life, but to speak candidly, I had moments of suicidal ideation, wondering if I'd be missed or if the kids would feel sad when I was gone. I realize how dramatic that sounds, but I was just a kid. I didn't have a way to process or deal with what I was feeling. This was actual trauma, and I never really worked through it, even in my twenties or thirties. I just covered my pain with busyness. My coping mechanism, as I grew older, was to perform in order to gain acceptance—at work, at church, with my parents, with my in-laws, with peer groups I tried to gain access to.

My complicated teenage trauma hangs on like a parasite, even in mid-life. Someone can make me feel forgotten or stupid, and my gut-level response is to run to my bedroom and cry. A while back, I applied for a ministry opportunity, and it seemed like it was a go. But then the call came: "We don't think you're the right fit for us." It didn't matter that the woman on the other end of the line was completely professional. Suddenly, the only thing that mattered was that I wasn't "the right fit." Her remarks loosed in me a fury of repressed insecurity. All I could hear were words the woman didn't actually say: *You're not good enough. We picked someone better. And it's not you.* Don't miss the irony of this. I spend countless hours encouraging other women to rest in God's love, yet that day I found myself alone in the kitchen, practically powerless under the tyranny of one sentence: "We don't think you're the right fit for us."

In a flash, the lie I believed is that I need people's approval to matter. When that happens, I get antsy and stressed out, thinking that if I work harder tomorrow, I'll get what I missed today. Next time, with enough effort, I'll be the one picked.

What does all this have to do with a Growing Slow mindset?

One of the reasons we are in a hurry is because we want to

know our life is mattering, and we're racing against time to make sure it will. In the rush, we substitute God's love with false imitations: accomplishment, a boyfriend, or a new Vera Bradley bag. We look for ways for the world to love us back, and the world will fall short. Every time.

I can't stop thinking about what would have happened if Jesus had operated that way. Jesus was pressed on every side and was often ridiculed or questioned. But Jesus didn't rush around trying to perform. Quite often, he told his friends to keep quiet about his miracles, and "he frequently withdrew to lonely places and prayed."[2] He surrounded himself with the love and direction of the Father, often in obscurity! Those moments with the Father centered him, placing him right in the middle of God's will.

What if the real reason we are in a hurry is because we've forgotten that we don't have to run in circles, chasing love?

Let's slow down. Let's have compassion for ourselves and ask God to heal our wounds, instead of trying to put Band-Aids over bullet holes. Let's accept where we are, resisting the urge to race forward in search of the mattering—because the mattering is right here.

Deep down, I think we are all a bunch of scared little kids. We are all dealing with some trauma from our past. We've all been hurt, and most of us probably haven't really dealt with the pain.

We have moments when we are sixteen years old on the inside, wanting to run to our bedrooms and cry it out. But we never do it. There's the pressure to keep pressing on, making the dinners, meeting the deadlines, putting one foot in front of the other. There's no time to cry or process. We have to intentionally build time into our lives so we can see that God is loving us, right here.

What if we were that intentional? What if, in a season of crisis or disappointment, we could all just go back to our bedrooms, flop onto our beds, and pound our fists into the mattress? What if we laid it all out before God: our pain, our failures, our neurotic attempts to control and fix, our past hurts?

This is where we will find God's love, like a surprise—by entering into the places where it hurts the most, instead of medicating with self-help, wine, Netflix, or Amazon Prime.

God makes it really clear: He is going to show up for us in our pain.

"He will not leave you or forsake you."[3]

"I am with you always, to the end of the age."[4]

For I am sure that neither death nor life, nor angels nor rulers, nor things present nor things to come, nor powers, nor height nor depth, nor anything else in all creation, will be able to separate us from the love of God in Christ Jesus our Lord.[5]

I could go on.

He is not going to leave you alone, at the homecoming dance, the school lunchroom, or wherever your wounds of unworthiness were first inflicted.

I am not going to try to make the truth more complicated than it is. The Sunday school answer is the right answer. The answer is Jesus.

For every hurt you're feeling, for every moment you feel obscure, for every second you've felt overlooked, for every time you have felt like the fields you're planting are weedy and unproductive, here stands Jesus, with his arms open wide. That's the only thing that is going to break this insanity of us feeding our need for love with sorry substitutes. We need to make ourselves sixteen again—or five, or twelve, or twenty-three, or thirty-eight, or whenever it was that we stopped believing God's love was enough for us. And then we need to look around to see where God was, even then.

I wish I could go back to sixteen-year-old Jennifer and tell her to look around, to see that Jesus was in the room with her when no one else saw her. He was there, sitting cross-legged at the end of her bed.

Often, when old insecurities rise up, I do battle with that awkward, insecure girl. In my shame, I don't know what to do with her besides scold her or ignore her. Maybe what I really need to do is send her into the arms of Jesus, who says, "Come here, girl. It's okay. I love you."

Could you do the same today?

Could you let Jesus meet the child in you? Could you let God reparent you?[6] Whenever you find yourself striving for love, could you look up and ask the Lord to hold you? When we hurt, we need a way for God to step in and be the dad who swoops up his little girl and reminds her that she is loved, loved, loved.

I've done a lot of dumb things for love. I've used up a lot of hairspray, dated too many of the wrong boys, racked up a lot of airline miles, said yes to a hundred committees—all in the name of love.

The smartest thing I ever did was open myself up to the love of Jesus.

That's it. If there is any good thing in me, it's the love of Jesus.

Do you need a love like that? You don't have to wait. You don't need to get to a certain age to get this whole thing figured out. That dawned on me recently, during a potluck dinner with friends. I'm a little embarrassed to tell you that my contribution had two cans of creamed soup in it, but then again, you'd need to try my mom's "Chicken on Sunday" before you judged it.

After dinner, we pushed aside the plates and settled in for conversation.

A friend tossed out a question, asking how he could rest his mind and set aside the cares of his work when he had so much responsibility to see it succeed.

Most of us at the table were in our forties, and because he was still in his twenties, we all gave him the easy answer. We kept telling him that it would get easier in time, as he aged. We all knew from experience what it was like to lose sleep on account of our ambition to grow beautiful and good things in the fields we'd been assigned. In time, he'd learn the art of Growing Slow.

True enough, as I've gotten older, my preference for slower-paced living has strengthened. It's become easier for me to resist the temptation of bigger and faster. Perhaps it's because I have also experienced some success in my life, and I know what it cost me. I don't want to say I regret what I've accomplished, but I know I paid a price.

After I got home from dinner that night, I couldn't help but feel regret over our advice. We should have never left him with the impression that he had to wait, that his feeling would "work itself out in time." Because you shouldn't have to wait! You shouldn't have to wait until you reach some magical age to settle the issue of worth and love and significance. Some things really aren't worth waiting for.

The next day, I called our friend. I felt like he needed a big sister. I told him that despite the gender difference, I was a lot like him: driven, ambitious, high capacity.

And then, I told him what I've been learning on my own Growing Slow journey. Ultimately, for me, this was a question of identity and love. I told him about the questions I had been asking myself:

Who am I?
What defines me?
What gives me worth?
Where do I find love and acceptance?

In the end, it's not my accomplishments or books. It's not even my family that gives me worth.

It's Jesus alone.

The whole point is Jesus and his willingness to give up his status in heaven, to become one of us down here on earth. Because of that, we have been invited into a relationship with him.

The Pharisees were all about trying to prove themselves to God. My friend and I would have been great Pharisees—meeting benchmarks, proving our worth. But God did away with all that proving. The whole narrative of the Bible hinges on people being unable to keep all the rules, so he made a way for us that invites us to come as we are: broken, weak, sixteen years old, crying, raging, unsteady, indecisive, prone to doubt. We wail, and he takes us back again.

Someday, I could lose my ability to write or communicate or deliver or achieve. I want to be okay if that happens. I want to know that I am not defined by "results."

I am defined by a singular relationship. That's it.

I am going to keep working hard. I am going to keep planting seeds and watching things grow.

And I will remember that there are some things worth waiting for, periods when we will have to wait for God to move, crops to grow, some prayer to be answered.

But we don't have to wait to find love. It's right here, right now.

Jesus is waiting. He is love. And love has been right here, all the time.

REMEMBER

Let Jesus meet the child in you.

REFLECT

Have you ever leaned on substitutes for God's love?

....

....

....

Imagine you are sixteen again—or five, or twelve, or twenty-three, or thirty-eight or whenever it was that you stopped believing God's love was enough for you. Can you find Jesus in the room? What would he say to you?

....

....

....

....

What are you defined by? Write the word or words below.

....

....

....

....

RETURN

At the end of each chapter,
we return to the soil.

I want you to remember: for every hurt you're feeling today, for every moment you feel obscure, for every second you've felt overlooked, for every time you have felt like the fields you're planting are weedy and unproductive, here stands Jesus, with his arms open wide. Write a prayer to Jesus, acknowledging that he is standing with you in your fields.

CHAPTER 10

GOOD FENCES

If I could lose my salvation, it would have happened the day a rogue pig showed up in our yard.

My hands were wrist-deep in dishwasher when I saw it out of the corner of my eye—a blur, a moving blob at first. And then I made out the figure as it scooted behind the shed, its pink rump shimmying in all its corpulent glory.

This immediately caused alarm for three reasons.

First, the pig was not ours, and it had clearly ventured far from home. Second, while I myself am a pig farmer's wife, I do not have the advanced pig herding skills that this task would require.

Third, as I surveyed the yard, it was quickly evident that the pig had made use of its rooting instinct. It had uprooted turf and soil hither and yon. Our yard looked like Swiss cheese.

This sent me out the door faster than you can say "pork chop."

I ran around the back side of the shed to find it digging another large hole in a beautiful patch of grass.

I had the sudden realization that I really had no idea what to do. I was no match for this pig. This wasn't a charming little Wilbur-type pig. This was a 250-pound beast who was about the right size to become bacon. It was as if the pig knew its days on earth were numbered, because it had quite the devil-may-care level of sass going on. Upon my arrival, the pig turned its snout in my general direction, cocked its head, gave me the side eye, then went back to its task of digging.

So I did what any sensible farmer's wife would do: I picked up a handful of landscaping rocks. I began hurling the rocks, one by one, at the pig, along with a string of obscenities, for which I have asked—and been granted—forgiveness from our Lord.

My attempts caused a minor disruption in the pig's plan. It picked up its snout and trotted off, with me chasing behind, hurling more rocks and choice words. Do you recall the moment in Scripture when Jesus sends some demons into a herd of pigs, and they all dramatically plunge off a cliff to their deaths? In my yard that afternoon, I was convinced that one of those pigs had gotten away and had been roaming the earth for the last two thousand-plus years with the sole aim of terrorizing me.

Pig v. Jennifer continued for approximately forever. And then it came to a halt when I made a catastrophic miscalculation. I grabbed a large stick and threw it with such force that a large splinter impaled the side of my hand.

I marched angrily up the side of the hill to remove the splinter, tend to my bleeding wound, take a deep breath, and text the neighbor to come fetch this barbaric, demon-possessed varmint.

The farmer immediately drove over, apologized profusely, and retrieved his animal. I am sure I terrified the poor man when he showed up to find blood streaming onto the driveway from my hand, a deranged look in my eye. We haven't spoken of it since, though we have exchanged pleasantries a number of times.

Title of this sob story: The Importance of Fences, An Essay.

In all honesty, the farmer—a longtime family friend—had fences. We also have fences. But sometimes, fences give way. Sometimes, they need mending. On a farm, fences are needed to keep some things in and other things out. We know firsthand the damage a trampling herd of stray cattle can do to a planted field—it's far worse than my Swiss-cheesed yard. Even raccoons can make quick work of a few rows of sweet corn after the sun goes down.

Fences are a way to take care of what we're growing on the farm.

They are also a way to take care of what you're growing in your *life*.

If you have a pet dog, you likely have a way to keep it fenced in. If you have a child, you're probably familiar with those clumsy safety gates that you have to practically hurdle over in order to access the stairs. If we are wise, we put fences around our families, our relationships, our calendars, our behaviors, our priorities, and our urges when we want to eat every carb in the house.

Don't mistake fences for walls. Walls can feel closed in and tight. I don't want you think that fences are the equivalent of crossing your arms across your chest, frowning like a curmudgeonly old man who yells at the neighbor kids, "Get off my lawn!"

Fences aren't intended to divide. Good fences *protect* and *preserve* the beautiful things you're growing.

Fences communicate your belief that your land holds life worthy of safeguarding.

I've had a messy relationship with fences, and I don't mean just that afternoon with the pig. One area I've needed fences is in my penchant to overcommit. I've been erecting fences which, if they could take a physical shape, would look like the letters N and O chain-linked together and wrapped around my life.

In this season of life, I've said no to more speaking engagements than I have during my decade of ministry. I have declined other opportunities that could have propelled me forward. As a church member, I no longer feel like I'm letting down the Lord if I don't sign up as frequently to bring snacks for our church's coffee hour. While I often say "yes," I have permission to say "no."

This doesn't mean I turn my back on ministry, the needy, the hungry, the hurting, the grieving, the committee seat, the next new book idea.

Fences help me see that this is my property and that is not; this is my responsibility and that is not. Fences mean that we don't give to every charity, but we do give generously to the ones God has purposely placed in our "field." We support local businesses and local ministries, like our church. It's small, tucked in between farm fields, but great things grow in small places with old wooden pews and hymnals.

For somebody who wants to run a million miles an hour, fences are a form of self-control. Furthermore, boundaries are biblical.

Like a city whose walls are broken through is a person who lacks self-control.[1]

Sometimes, we need others to show us where our fences need mending, or to reveal places where we have no fences at all. Perhaps you could call on a spiritual mentor, a trusted friend, or a counselor to help you see your fences more clearly.

Emily P. Freeman would tell you that we could all benefit from this kind of person, whom she calls a "No Mentor." She says that ideally, your No Mentor should be someone who makes decisions the way you would want to make them, someone who is straightforward and unapologetic. This person probably has reliable, sturdy fences. "A No Mentor is there to help you feel confident about saying no to the things you really don't want to do anyway or to help you finally discover your strong, brave yes in the midst of fear."[2]

Like farmers whose fields are separated by fences, your fences will define where your responsibility ends and someone else's begins. This is also important as you consider the boundaries required in personal relationships. You can set limits and be a loving person at the same time.

The temptation will be to widen fences, to move the posts out a little further so you can plant more seeds and perhaps produce a bigger harvest. There may well come a time to widen your reach, your scope, your influence. But friend, may I encourage you to let the Lord move the fences, and not the people who are telling you that you need to take it to the next level?

I see you—the girl in high school, who feels pressure to widen the fence posts and figure out what you plan to do with the rest of your life when you're just trying to navigate the complex world of being a teen.

I see you—the single woman at the restaurant, who feels pressure to find a guy and settle down, even though you are enjoying the beautiful things you are growing on your own.

I see you—the newlywed wife, in your car at the stoplight. Already, people are asking you when you plan to have a baby, but you are enjoying these first sweet years of marriage, and frankly, you're not sure if parenthood will be a part of your future.

I see you—the mama at the park, who feels the pressure to have another, and maybe two more after that, but you just want to take it easy for a while.

There's always something more, something out there to be learned, accomplished, grown, achieved—as if widening your fences makes you a complete woman.

A bigger field won't complete you.

Another accomplishment won't complete you.

A heftier paycheck won't complete you.

A higher yield won't complete you.

You are free to see yourself as a complete, whole person, no matter what you're growing these days.

Fences are a way of taking care of yourself, just as you are, not as anyone else thinks you should be. Make no mistake: it's your God-given right to simply abide in the place where he has placed you for this moment in history. Rest. Sit still. Tend to the matters at hand. Marvel at the slow growth beneath your feet, just as the Lord surely marvels at the way he is growing you—as a flower gently unfolds on a summer morning, after a long night of rain.

For He Loved the Soil

The story of Uzziah illustrates both the blessing and pitfall of growing good things over time.

Uzziah's story can be found in the midst of a long line of kings whose stories are told through Scripture. The Bible identifies kings as good or terrible. The determining factor is how they were seen in the eyes of the Lord. Terrible kings "did evil in the eyes of the Lord."[3] But good kings "did what was right in the eyes of the Lord."[4]

Uzziah became king when he was only sixteen years old, and like his dad, he "did what was right in the eyes of the Lord,"[5] which is the equivalent of a high five from God.

Like us, Uzziah had decisions to make about what he was growing, raising, digging, and building. During his life, Uzziah built towers, dug cisterns, and owned livestock in the foothills and on the plains. He had people working his fields and vineyard in the fertile land, "for he loved the soil."[6]

I am fond of that phrase. *For he loved the soil.*

I imagine young Uzziah looking out on his fertile fields in the morning, with the sun rising over the horizon, pulling out his iPhone, snapping a photo, and posting it on Instagram with the caption: "Guys, I love the soil. #Kingsofinstagram #nofilter"

From the overflow of his love for the soil, Uzziah stewarded its care and employed people to tend to it. At various points in his journey, Uzziah pushed out his proverbial fences. This wasn't all bad. Certain times and opportunities call us to broaden our influence,

widen our embrace, take risks, and do what we thought we could never do. It worked out well for Uzziah.

"His fame spread far and wide, for he was greatly helped until . . ."

Wait for it.

. . . "until he became powerful."[7]

Growth can be a tremendous blessing, but it can also lead any of us—even the greatest of kings—to become puffed up with pride.

Pride led to Uzziah's downfall. He showed up at the temple one day, demanding that he be allowed to burn the incense on the altar. The priests didn't appreciate how he planned to usurp their authority, and apparently the Lord didn't, either. Uzziah was seized by leprosy and forced to live in a separate house until his death.

Uzziah's story had a promising start and a tragic ending. He loved the soil, but in the end, he loved power more.

Uzziah needed better fences around his motivations and his heart.

As you think about the fences in your life, remember that some are there to keep toxic things out. They are also a way to hem you in. This is God's way of stewarding us. He could obliterate all the fences and let your growth run like wild vines across the hillsides, but he has you right where you are for a reason.

And if a stray pig comes by for a visit, try asking the Google machine what to do. I have no idea how to help you.

REMEMBER

Fences communicate your
belief that your land holds life
worthy of safeguarding.

REFLECT

How well-defined are your boundaries?

....

....

In what area of your life are your fences in need of
mending?

....

....

Have you ever had a "No Mentor"? Do you think you
could use one? Why or why not?

....

....

....

....

RETURN

The pig in my yard had found a weak spot in a fence, which resulted in the pig digging holes in my yard. Has a weak boundary in your life ever resulted in damage to you or someone you love? What can you do today to mend a fence or erect a new one? That might look like saying no to an opportunity, lengthening the distance between you and a toxic person, or refusing to yield to the pressure to move to the next level.

CHAPTER 11

THE ONE WHERE WE GROW
SLOW WITH FRIENDS

In my experience, here's what suffers most in the chaos of a rushed existence: relationships. Hurry wounds the bonds of connection.

We can't connect with our kids when we are constantly trying to rush them out of the house to the next activity. We can't connect with a spouse when we are so distracted that we can't pause long enough to look him in the eye. We can't connect with our friends when, while they're laying out the options for a girls' day out, we're calculating the risk of being gone from the office that long.

A life of hurry places resumes above relationships, performance over people, and achievement over affection. The most rushed seasons of my life accidentally hardened my heart to the real needs of real people in my life. In recent years, this awareness shifted something in me. When I am tempted to return to hasty living, God rearranges my heart by bringing this quote to mind: "People will forget what you said. People will forget what you did. But people will never forget how you made them feel."[1]

I have only wanted people to feel loved. It breaks my heart to think how my accelerated existence may have left people feeling like they had a run-in with a porcupine.

With a Growing Slow mindset, un-hurried hearts soften to rediscover a fondness for what matters most: true connection.

I have a story for you about true connection. And it begins with that awkward first step of invitation. I hope you'll notice that a story like this could never happen in a hurry. It takes time, intention, and even some risk.

Come with me to a house on a hill, under the bluest Iowa summer sky.

A House with a Name

Most people wouldn't have bothered naming the house, but then again, Kim and Wayne Van Dyke aren't like most people. Their farmhouse was a gigantic, white-sided, black-shuttered hulk of a house. Yet somehow, she had a heart.

Kim and Wayne knew that for sure.

And the way they figured it, whatever had a heart needed a name.

To be really clear about the whole thing, Wayne knew it first. He knew it clear as the June sky that arced over his farmland. This house that held what he treasured most—his wife and two daughters—it needed the perfect name.

He said they got her "for a song" in 1997. They couldn't have afforded the house on their own. They credited God's unmerited favor, which most of us call "grace."

You might say the house was a bit like heaven, the sort of place you could never sneak into by pulling up your own bootstraps or paying off the guy who watches over the place. No one earns something like that. It's only grace.

But the name for this house? It just wasn't coming to Wayne. He needed to take his time.

Mothers know this, how you have to sometimes hold your newborn in your arms a while, inspecting their pug noses and half-open eyelids and dimpled chins to know whether you've just birthed a Herbie or a Helmer.

So that's how it might have been with Wayne. Morning by morning, he sat at his Formica table, thinking about a name. He asked for God's help. He spread open those marked-up Bible pages, praying gospel-hard with a Merit Menthol wedged between his lips, like maybe he could send smoke signals to the angels. Wayne sipped his Folgers coffee—inky black with a smidgen of sugar.

One morning, it came to him, like a voice thundering down through the roof. He'd swear to you that he heard it audibly: "Name her Grace."

He smushed out his cigarette in the ashtray and went to the bedroom to tell his wife.

Yes, God had said to name her Grace. But Wayne took one small liberty when he shook his wife awake: "She's Gracie."

Before Gracie, there was the Stone Pony. The Stone Pony was the cinder block house where the family had lived for years. Bat wings tap-tapped against the cinder blocks. Winter exhaled in frosty breaths of lace, straight up the walls. The girls' babysitters never took their coats off.

Wayne and Kim and the girls prayed and prayed for a new house. But everything seemed too big or too small or too expensive. They prayed some more. Then, Gracie came on the market. She was an eighty-year-old parsonage that would need to be moved. It seemed like a long shot, but Wayne and Kim bid on the house. They were the only bidders.

Gracie was theirs. But first, they would need to burn down the beloved Stone Pony to make room for Gracie.

Kim and the girls were sad to see flames licking the sides of the Stone Pony, but Wayne? He crossed his arms over his chest and quipped, "Well, that's the warmest that house has ever been."

Then they moved Gracie in place, like a queen come home. She was glorious. She was warm on the cold days and cool on the hot ones.

And she was huge.

Wayne and Kim knew that Gracie ought to be shared. They couldn't keep a gift like that to themselves. So they pulled a yellow legal pad from the kitchen drawer and started writing down the names of people. The list of names included the hurting, the healed, the healthy, the harried, the hurried, and the maybe a little bit hopeless. Everyone on the list had something in common: their souls needed grace and connection.

Wayne and Kim wanted to have guests over—whoever, whenever, and as often as possible—mostly, it seemed, on Saturday nights.

Every Saturday morning, over steaming cups of Folgers (but no more cigarettes; Wayne quit), Kim and Wayne pulled out the legal pad. Whoever was at the top of the list got a call. They would go down the list, calling until they found someone who was free for supper.

The guests came through the door—some of them tentative, hugging themselves—and found a seat at the table. They ate simple food off of simple pottery. This wasn't a Pinterest showcase. This was gospel hospitality.

They'd talk about rain or crops or the headlines.

And they'd always, always talk about Jesus. Wayne wouldn't have it any other way. He was a gospel man, a prophetic voice, and some may bristle at such a forward way of sharing the faith, but Wayne never wanted to miss the opportunity to share the best news he'd ever heard with whomever sat at his table.

Often, before the guests left, they'd all eat ice cream the "Wayne Way"—vanilla ice cream, chocolate syrup, milk, and malt powder on top.

And so it went for years. More people came. More friends heard about grace while sitting inside Gracie.

After supper one June night, Wayne Van Dyke, age fifty-two, dished himself up a final bowl of ice cream, the "Wayne Way."

The next morning, it was Saturday—time to pull out the legal pad. Kim stretched awake first and blurred her way toward the coffee pot. She made the Folgers. Did her devotions. Prayed. And waited.

Fifteen minutes had passed, and still, Wayne hadn't come to the table. He had always risen to the smell of coffee.

"The moment I touched his shoulder I knew he had gone to heaven," Kim said.

Within hours, all those friends who'd eaten the ice cream, drank the coffee, heard the gospel, prayed the prayers, sung the hymns, pulled a chair up to the Formica . . . they all showed up. With lasagna and paper plates and five kinds of Jell-O and the longest hugs and rivers of tears and no-words-just-no-words-at-all and grace upon grace upon grace. They all showed up.

It was a June day when folks said goodbye to Wayne. Everyone piled onto Gracie's lap with lawn chairs and memories and laughter and spilling-over grief. They had the service in the yard, sang songs, and told stories.

And up above them—past that arc of blue Iowa sky where birds in Vs passed over in their mysterious flights and where the June sun eased its rays down on their cheeks and where angels dwell—grace carried Wayne all the way home.

Kim told me that the best part of the day was at the cemetery, in the moment when she looked across the casket to see all of the guys Wayne loved most: his Christian community.

"Love held me together at that moment," she said.

This is how we do the friend thing: we slow down enough to hold each other together with love. But we first extend the awkward invitation—maybe even as awkward as scrawling a list of names on a legal pad.

Taking the first step toward connection is almost always awkward. Just ask Ruth, whose awkward first date started when she slept on the floor at the feet of Boaz. Or Zacchaeus, who climbed out of a tree to have supper with Jesus. Or any startled, first-century Christian who met Saul in the first few days after the former persecutor assured them all that he was now one of them.

There are no life hacks for connection. Relationships don't just "happen." The awkward first step is key. We invite someone to dinner, to church, or to sit next to us on the bleachers. Whatever it takes. We simply must slow down enough to make the first move—not waiting for them to go first—and then we push that invitation, like a seed, into the soil of connection. And then we water the seed and wait. Those first awkward moves aren't limited to inviting strangers, like Wayne and Kim did. It's also the first awkward move to say you're sorry, to mend the wound, to reestablish contact with someone you still care for deeply but have neglected for a long time.

True connection takes time, effort, and patience.

For example, when Scott and I started dating in 1993, I had a hunch almost immediately that he was my forever love. I'd never felt that way about anyone before. But you don't start planning a wedding after the first date. The falling-in-love part was the easy part. We needed to learn what it meant to *stay* in love. We needed to have enough courage to grow slow together, to learn what it meant to compromise, forgive, deal with conflict, bend, and trust. We dated for three years before we said, "I do." The way of Growing Slow helped us put down strong, deep roots that would keep us steady in the storms and trials that would inevitably come.

It's the same way a corn plant—with its roots that go way down deep—can survive an Iowa windstorm that can bend the plant clean over. Quite often, that plant will miraculously pop back up after a few days. It's all because of the roots.

You simply can't put down roots quickly. And you cannot

connect and hurry at the same time. Not with a boyfriend. Not with a child, who needs you to get down to their level, look them in the eye, and really listen. Not with your elderly neighbor, who would give anything for you to stop by and sip tea with her some Saturday afternoon.

People are starving for connection, but we are racing by, not even waving from the car window. We are avoiding eye contact at the store, sending off hasty text messages as a means of communication, and settling for shallow, fragile relationships because we don't even know what we're missing.

Let's be intentional. Let's be the people who grow slow with friends and with family, with strangers and with the new kid on the block. Let's reconnect with the people we've regrettably lost touch with, and then plant new seeds in rejoined hearts.

True connection will un-hurry a heart in ways that little else can.

One bright day, you'll know that those slow-grown roots took hold because there's growth above the soil.

Intentional connection. Deep roots. That's how we grow slow with friends and with Christ.

You're deeply rooted in him. You're well-constructed upon him. You know your way around the faith. Now do what you've been taught. School's out; quit studying the subject and start *living* it![2]

REMEMBER

You can't connect and hurry
at the same time.

REFLECT

How does a hurried heart make connection difficult for people?

....
....

Think of a time when someone's brusque nature, even if it was unintentional, made you feel bad. How can you make sure you don't give off the same brusque vibe?

....
....

....

How has an awkward beginning turned into true connection in your life?

....
....

....
....

RETURN

At the end of each chapter,
we return to the soil.

After Wayne died, hundreds of friends showed up and plopped their lawn chairs right down on the earth, in front of a big house named Gracie. In the blanks provided, make a list of people who have been a "Wayne" or "Kim" to you. Make a second list of the names of people to whom you would like to extend an invitation to connect.

PART 3

AUTUMN HARVEST

This is how it is with the kingdom of God;
it is as if a man were to scatter seed on the
land and would sleep and rise night and day
and the seed would sprout and grow, he
knows not how. Of its own accord the land
yields fruit, first the blade, then the ear, then
the full grain in the ear. And when the grain
is ripe, he wields the sickle at once, for the
harvest has come.

JESUS OF NAZARETH

CHAPTER 12

WHEN A DREAM DIES

Harvest has mercifully arrived on our farm, and when I think back to the struggle we faced in planting, I am even more convinced that the act of growing anything is both sacred and miraculous.

Harvest is one of the most beautiful seasons of all. Whether you are harvesting crops or ideas or efforts, there is nothing quite so satisfying as holding that fully ripened thing in your hand and relishing all that went into its growth. The planting of seeds, the watering, the waiting, the prayers, the perseverance, the weeding, the tending, the jaw-dropping moment when—against all odds—your seeds burst forth from hard ground to bear fruit that lasts.

As I scan the cornfield in front of the house, I see the blessing in it. The blessing is, of course, the fruit of these yellowed rows of crops, the color of a lion's mane swaying in an autumn breeze. Soon, farmers will work around the clock to reap what they've sown.

But along with the relief and satisfaction, harvest time can bring sadness, no matter what you're growing. For some, the sadness comes in knowing that everything you've worked so hard for is now completed. You wonder what's next.

For others, the sadness comes because the harvest doesn't look the way you expected.

For us, this harvest is a mix of both blessing and heartache. I feel the heartache every time I see that huge bald spot in the middle of the field in front of our house. It's a place where crops should have been planted but weren't because the ground was too wet to access. That part of the field looks like a giant wound, a reminder that this planting season, all was not well.

I confess, it feels like a sort of vandalism, like Mother Nature worked tirelessly to destroy the perennial hope of the farmer.

I'll bet you know what it feels like to look out on what God has given you and see a wound in the fields.

These are the places where dreams have died.

What dreams have died for you?

How have the harvest times in your life looked different than you expected?

Perhaps you are dealing with infertility. Divorce. Job loss. Financial distress. Rejection. Chronic pain. A called-off engagement. A loved one who refuses to communicate with you. An injury that set you back in your athletic career.

Especially agonizing is this: when your dream busts apart, inches from your promised land. You saw it with your eyes—a land flowing with milk and honey—and you were certain it was God's will for your life, but everything stalled out.

When I think about stalled-out dreams in a season of harvest, I think of Moses. He devoted his life to the work of leading the Israelites toward the promised land. When they finally arrived, Moses was an old man, but he wasn't allowed to set foot in the place he'd worked so hard to reach. He was only granted a view of it. Moses stood on Mount Nebo, overlooking the land, but the hand of God held him back. God told Moses that he'd not cross the Jordan to "enter the good land."[1]

Has there been a time in your life when the "good land" stretched out before you, but you weren't able to enter it? Have you felt the confusion that follows when you walk toward your dream, believing each obedient step is lined up with God's divine will, only to find yourself standing on your own Mount Nebo, watching your dream fade into the distance?

I have felt this kind of pain. Snatched-away dreams have wrecked me: bruised relationships, negative pregnancy tests, a slicing betrayal, a verbally abusive boss at my "dream job," a seriously ill child, disappointments in my career, a stack of rejections from publishers over the years.

In the playback, I see how God picked up the smashed pieces and rearranged them into a mosaic of unforeseen beauty. God doesn't always give us what we want in our personal seasons of harvest, but he's distinguished himself as sovereign, giving us *what we actually need*. Consider Lazarus outside his tomb, resurrected in front of his grieving friends, who had attended his funeral a few days before—a funeral Jesus had missed. Deep disappointment preceded a dazzling, divine drama.

The most astonishing such drama unfolded in the life, death, and resurrection of Jesus Christ. Consider Jesus in the Garden of Gethsemane, with blood on his brow, asking God to take a cup of suffering away from him, then uttering one of the most exacting prayers of all time: "Not my will, but yours be done."[2]

The very next day, Jesus' friends stood in anguish as every hope and dream spilled down Calvary in a torrent of sorrow. Three days later, Jesus bodily walked out of his own grave.

Only God can resurrect life from a dream that has died so horrifically. God's promise is that "all the broken and dislocated pieces of the universe—people and things, animals and atoms—get properly fixed and fit together in vibrant harmonies, all because of his death, his blood that poured down from the cross."[3]

Perhaps you are dwelling in the field of a dying dream. It might be hard to believe that any good thing will grow up from this hard ground.

Even though the harvest isn't what you thought, the harvest is still here. The Lord of the Harvest is always working many steps ahead of us, and what he has produced in and through us is not always immediately evident.

In Romans 8:28, God says that he works for the good of those who love him "in all things"—not just some things.

God is not partially sovereign.

He is not partially faithful.

He is not mostly good.

He is not halfway powerful.

He is not moderately loving.

He is all—and all in all.

This is the field where God is doing the slow work of growing us, bending low and tending our souls in the middle of our sobbing, begging, and pleading prayers. You don't have to be strong here. Choose to let yourself be weak. Fall into the arms of the Savior who wept at the tomb of Lazarus.

It is a sacred gift to discover Jesus walking with us, 'round the wounds of our fields, cupping the seeds of suffering in his own nail-scarred hands. Jesus suffers with us, just as he suffered for us.

You are not forgotten when the harvest looks different than you dreamed.

How We Cope with the Death of Dreams

I am the Queen of Unexpressed Grief, and I cope by hiding myself in productivity. This, of course, returns me to the toxicity of a hurried heart. Not only do I deny my heart the time it needs to feel what it needs to feel, but I cram it with deadlines and stress.

In the midst of grief and suffering, people fall into one of three categories: *do, think,* or *feel.*

Do. Doers busy themselves with productivity to mask disappointment. Of the three categories, doers are the quickest to adopt a new dream, which can be healthy. But they are also the most likely to stuff their feelings, and later, have a meltdown or an anxiety attack because they never dealt with the disappointment head on.

Think. Thinkers analyze and process. They investigate what worked well and question what they could have done differently. They cope by getting lost in the comfort of their own thoughts of how to "figure things out." Their intellectual journey may keep them from actually feeling what they need to feel, and they may be prone to internalize. They might describe themselves as "dead inside," or emotionless. Ultimately, they'll have to open the door to their closed-off feelings in order to truly heal.

Feel. Feelers lay it all on the table and let every shuddering tear fall. Feelers understand that joy and sorrow and anger and apathy and confusion and fear can coexist in the same body. The potential drawback, of course, is that they will forever believe everything they feel or think. But the truth is this: our emotions are release valves, not steering wheels.

I want to take a moment to focus on the lessons we can learn from Feelers about healthy living.

Can we all just agree to feel what we need to feel for a while?

When our harvest dreams die, I suppose that each of us eventually makes our way through all of the categories, but we gravitate toward one of the three. My downfall is that I avoid the feeling, and bury myself in the doing. I cover pain with metrics and pretending. In my most corrupted moments, I'll even hide behind my kids' achievements. If they've succeeded, somehow that reflects on my worth as a mom, or it makes up for the things I could never accomplish.

When all of that fails—and I assure you, it eventually does—we find ourselves disrobed of our coping mechanisms. Here, we finally must encounter our despair and release our unshed tears.

Does this sound familiar to you?

If you are standing on the edge of your promised land, and you can't "enter the good land," do you rush on to plant new seeds in a new field? If so, in what ways is your seed-planting actually an attempt to bury past pain deep down in the dark? If anybody has ever had a rebound boyfriend, you know exactly what I'm talking about.

Because we are a culture in a hurry, we rush to dream a new dream. But some things can't be rushed. Most things must be grown slow, including seeds of sorrow.

Grief takes time.

"Moving on" takes time.

Processing takes time.

Coming to terms with what happened takes time.

Maybe you need permission today to feel your feelings and take the time you need to move through disappointment. Stay in your unyielding fields for a little while longer. It will make the fruit that does eventually grow all that much sweeter.

How to Grow Slow in Grief

So how do we do it? How do we grow slow through intangible losses? There are no funerals for broken dreams.

When a person dies, it's obvious to everyone why you're sad. People will check in on you. They'll bring casseroles and ask how you're doing. They'll send sympathy cards. There are no good cards for dead dreams.

Many churches have a special time set aside on Sunday morning for prayer requests. People tend to ask for prayers for sick family members, safe travels, an upcoming medical appointment, or grieving friends. Rarely does someone ask for prayer for a more intangible heartbreak that needs to be grieved. If they did, it would go down like this:

"Can y'all pray that my daughter will return my calls? She hasn't talked to me for months."

"Would you mind praying for my mental state? I got fired from my dream job last Wednesday."

"Will you say a prayer for my dad? He started drinking again."

Of course, there are valid reasons that keep us from sharing so vulnerably—privacy being one. But my point is this: almost everyone is carrying around an intangible loss, and there's a good chance they haven't really figured out how to process it.

When a dream dies, you not only lose hope, but you can feel isolated and shut off. In that lonely place, it's tempting to rank our pain and compare it to someone else's. You might cope with a broken dream by convincing yourself it shouldn't hurt as much as it does. You might even blame yourself.

See if either of these phrases resonates:

"It's my fault it didn't work out."
"I should have tried harder."

Some of the worst fallout happens when we "at least" ourselves, or when others "at least" us, for example:

"It could be worse. At least you didn't die."

I hereby propose a resolution in which we strike the non-empathetic "at leasts" from the language we use to address anyone's pain, including our own.

When someone's child is sick, it is not helpful to say, "At least she's alive."

When someone's child dies, it's not helpful to say, "At least you have two other kids."

When someone has a miscarriage, it's not helpful to say, "At least this didn't happen after she was born."

When someone gets cancer, it's not helpful to say, "At least you didn't get _____ type of cancer. That's much worse."

When someone loses a job, it's not helpful to say, "At least you're still employable."

One reason some people don't share their heartaches openly at prayer time is because they know they will get at-leasted to death.

I have probably at-leasted someone out there. I know I have at-leasted myself, and when I do, I accidentally minimize the pain by comparing it to something "worse."

Un-hurrying our hearts means we sit with our feelings, instead of running from them, comparing them, or at-leasting them.

A few good practices as we grow slow in grief:

Talk it out
Cry
Ask for help
Write down what hurts
Reflect

This is part of Growing Slow through grief.

I know this might sound weird, but what if we held little funerals for dead dreams? You could do that. Go ahead. Play a song. Say a prayer. Deliver a eulogy. Whatever you need to do to deal with the kind of grief no one really talks about.

Friend, it's okay to grieve a shredded dream. Your life has been upended.

If you're like me, you don't want to wallow in those sad feelings forever. You want to feel like you'll be able to move on at some point.

Try this. First name your emotion. "Right now, I feel _____."
Then, give yourself a time limit to feel that emotion. A counselor
once told me to give negative emotions a time limit—for instance,
I will let myself be angry until one o'clock or until next Friday or
whatever—and then let it go. It doesn't always work for everybody
or for every sorrow, but it's a place to start.

When the time is right—and you'll know when it is—you can
dare to dream again.

REMEMBER

Most things must be grown slow,
including seeds of sorrow.

REFLECT

Consider the harvest seasons of your life. What is the
most beautiful harvest you've ever experienced?

....

....

....

What was the hardest harvest, one wherein a dream
died?

....

....

....

Of the three categories of grief (see page 129), do you
tend to lean toward doing, thinking, or feeling?

....

....

....

What do you think the difference is between wallowing
in grief and Growing Slow in grief?

....

....

....

RETURN

At the end of each chapter,
we return to the soil.

In the Lee fields, harvest brought blessing next to heartache—harvestable crops next to a gigantic wound where we couldn't plant anything in the spring. Joy and sorrow can coexist in one field, and they can coexist in one heart. How has your heart held conflicting emotions?

CHAPTER 13

YOU ARE ALLOWED
TO CHANGE

Friends thought we lost our minds when we moved back to the farm.

Scott had graduated with a law degree and was making strides in his career with an insurance company. I was on my way to living out the dream I had been chasing since my freshman year of college. When we announced our decision to leave the city, a colleague told me I was making a terrible mistake. He said I was throwing away all the experience and clout I had earned over the years by moving to "Hickville."

So be it. We followed a moving truck to a place that, we hoped, would be our own little promised land on the western edge of Iowa. But don't think for a moment that we didn't worry our critics were right. To be honest, I was terrified.

We all have this idea about growth, and it goes something like this: Once you plant seeds in a certain field, you ought to stick around long enough to reap the harvest. You don't leave when it's about to get good.

Maybe it looks like this for you:

You picked a college major based on a presumed career path. Junior year, you are tugged in a new direction but fear you will lose traction if you reroute.

You said "yes" to the marriage proposal. Now, you feel a growing unease that he is not the right guy for you, but you fear the shame and loneliness of calling off the wedding.

You are moving forward in your career, and everyone says you have great potential if you keep up the pace, but you can't shake the feeling that you're less interested in climbing the ladder and more interested in slowing it down.

Here's what we all need to know: even though we may plant seeds in a particular course of study, a community, a ministry, a relationship, a career path, that doesn't mean we have to stick around to see the harvest.

You are allowed to move to a new field where you will plant different seeds. You are allowed to change.

We all know how hard change can be. Many of us avoid change because of fear. We worry about how people will react. We worry that change will actually bring us more pain. And we wonder whether we are squandering the effort we put into fields we already planted.

But as Kristen Strong wrote in *Girl Meets Change*, "If we want to not be afraid of life, we need to hold inside us a flexible spirit."[1]

I have not always had a flexible spirit. I'll remind you that I lived in the same house, attended the same church, and had the same friends my entire childhood.

As an adult, I realized my learned pattern of sameness had the potential to hold me back. In 1998, I was offered a newspaper job I didn't actually apply for. I was already happily working at another newspaper. After making a lengthy pros and cons list with my husband—the way we've made almost every major decision as a married couple—we decided to move.

The day we made the decision, I stuck a Post-It note on my desk with the words, "Change is good." More than two decades later, the note is still right here, next to my keyboard. It's faded by years of exposure to the sun.

I keep the note because I need to remember that the best decisions I've made in my life required change and risk.

I'm allowed to change, and so are you.

You are allowed to change your mind. You are allowed to change your college major. You are allowed to change your group of friends when it's clear they aren't healthy for you anymore.

You are allowed to change your passions and dreams, trading them in for a fresh idea of how you want to live your one precious life.

You are allowed to adopt a new plan, take a new job, or venture down a different path.

You are allowed to start over.

As the years go by, we learn that the things we were certain about when we were seventeen feel a little less certain at age thirty-five. We don't have to apologize for that.

We don't have to be ashamed, or feel guilty, or wonder if there's something wrong with us when we make a 180-degree turn. Change is how we grow. Change is how we become the people God truly made us to be.

And even though we won't see the harvest in those first fields, that doesn't mean we won't see a harvest. Planting seeds produces inner growth that we carry with us for the rest of our lives, no matter where we roam.

That growth impacts both what we do and who we are.

What We Do

When we moved to the farm, we were still paying off law school debt. We quietly wondered if those three years of school had been squandered. But we now see the harvest. Scott earned a specialized degree in agricultural law, and he now uses it to make decisions on the farm. Meanwhile, I thought my writing life would flatline after our move. Blogs weren't even a thing when we moved to the farm, and book writing wasn't my style. I liked the short-term gratification of cranking out a short story for the next day's paper. The idea of spending more than a year writing 55,000 words in a book never crossed my mind.

But here we are, seeing the harvest of what we planted in other fields, long ago.

Take a moment to consider this question: How have seeds planted long ago brought about a harvest in what you're doing in the current season of your life?

Who We Are

The more important growth happens within. When I consider times I've experienced God's faithfulness most profoundly, it was never when I felt most comfortable or secure in my own abilities. Instead, it was in moments when God called me out of every comfort zone, every rut of mediocrity, every cove of security. Yes, our souls grow in fields of plenty, but they also flourish when we step into the great unknown, trusting not in our own might but entirely in our Savior.

Do you sense God calling you into a new season, a new field, or a new land?

What would it be like to leave what feels comfortable, to have a flexible spirit, to embrace the unknown? Perhaps, for now, you are called to stay. But don't discount a change simply because you don't want to leave what's comfortable.

Change Takes Courage

One of my favorite examples of this kind of courage is found in the story of Abram.

You could say that Little Abe was a city kid, growing up in Ur of the Chaldeans, a flourishing city of wealthy, educated people. The Bible drops hints that Abram's family worshipped other gods in that metropolis where idolatry was rampant. Hebrew tradition even suggests that Abram's father had an idol shop, and that Abram took to smashing some of the idols with a hammer.

It's evident that Abram's heart was open to something other than an idol-worshipping lifestyle, because as Abram grew older, God picked him, out of everyone else on the planet, and gave him directions for his future.

"Leave your country, your people, and your father's household and go to the land I will show you."[2]

Let's pause for a moment and consider what was at stake here. First of all, Abram was no spring chicken. Scripture tells us that he was seventy-five years old when God asked him to leave everything familiar and comfortable: his home, his work, his family, the places and people that had shaped who he was up until that point in his life.

God promised Abram great things, but Abram would have to make a huge change in order to grab hold of those promises.

The risk was high. Note that God didn't tell Abram where he was heading. He only told him to leave for "the land I will show you."

Abram's obedience to this call is evident in a short, three-word sentence:

So Abram went.[3]

Because of his obedience, Abram experienced the promised blessings of God. God gave him a new name—Abraham—made a covenant with him, and promised to make a nation of his descendants. Abraham would be fruitful and blessed.

Imagine if Abraham had refused to embrace change. Imagine if he had sought comfort over calling. His decision could have altered the course of history in devastating ways. But the fruit of his obedience unfolds powerfully in the very first sentence of the New Testament:

> Jesus Christ came from the family of King David and also from the family of Abraham.[4]

Is God calling you to a new land?

Like my Post-It note says, "change is good." But that doesn't mean it's easy.

Change can be extremely hard. Change can taste like salt in your tears. It can look like an expansive wilderness that lies before you as you leave your own "Ur," setting out for the land God will show you.

Sometimes we change our lives, and sometimes our lives change us. But the biggest changes always happen on the inside, during that expansive interior journey where God asks each of us to move our hearts out of their precious comfort zones.

God causes us to reconsider our stubborn positions and to see this beautiful and broken world from other vantage points. As for me and my family, we hope we've done that. We're still learning. We've been known to trip over our own two feet. But we hope that the changes we've made have, in turn, made us better versions of ourselves.

That is our prayer, and time will tell.

How about you? What change feels especially risky for you today?

Is God calling you to a "land [he] will show you"? If so, dare to venture forth from the fields that feel safe, so you can experience the goodness of God in a whole new way, in a whole new place.

Let's test it, to feel the Rock beneath our feet in a new land, with new people or new experiences. Perhaps, in the "land [he] will show you," you will learn something surprising about our shared humanity, common dignity, greater justice, deeper kindness.

Yeah, change is hard. But change can also be good, even if it goes bad—because God can work it for good, for his glory. I have to believe that, or I might never take another risk and embrace the place God has for me tomorrow.

A Change of Scenery

A few years after we moved here, I submitted an opinion essay to my old newspaper editor about moving back to the farm, leaving behind the harvest promised in the city.

I wrote:

> Growing up, I didn't notice. Never batted an eye when the sun melted like orange sherbet over the fields in my backyard. Never looked twice when the grass sprouted a green, lush carpet under my bare toes. Only now, as I write it all down, do I remember that an early winter rain could turn a clothesline into a chandelier.
>
> I didn't notice the beauty of a whole lot of things—like how death can be breathtaking. Have you ever seen the hopeful allure of a dying farm field in October?
>
> Maybe it takes a change of scenery to remember what you didn't see the first time around.
>
> I do remember when I told that farm boy that I'd never, ever, ever move back to rural Iowa with him.
>
> I also remember the day I had a change of heart; I was sitting on our bathroom floor with my arms cradling a swelling belly of new life. I don't know who was more surprised when I told the farm boy that we should move back home.

After I submitted the essay, I got an email from my former editor. He confessed, "I always shook my head at your decision to move to the farm and leave reporting." But, he added, after reading the essay, "I found answers to all of those 'why did she' questions I uttered years ago. And when I read the references to 'that farm boy,' I just smiled as my eyes dampened. It all makes perfect sense now."

It might not make sense to you in the moment. It might not make sense to your neighbor, your father-in-law, your college professor, your boss, or your friends.

It might not make sense now, but someday, I believe, it will. For now, let's trust that it all makes sense to God.

REMEMBER

Change is how we grow.

REFLECT

Are you change-averse, or does change excite you?
Why?

....
....
....
....

Have you felt the sting of disapproval when you chose a
new path? If so, how?

....
....
....
....
....

What change in your life has been most impactful?

....
....
....
....
....

RETURN

At the end of each chapter,
we return to the soil.

In Genesis, God gave Abram simple instructions: "Go."
Simple to say, harder to do. Do you feel God calling you
to "go"? If so, write a prayer here asking for the strength
to have the faith of Abram.

....

....

....

....

....

....

....

....

....

....

....

....

....

....

....

....

....

....

....

CHAPTER 14

THE THING WE'RE
MOST AFRAID OF

O ne warm autumn day, several years ago, Scott drove the old green combine up the driveway at the farm as his father looked on. If you don't know what a combine is, picture a gigantic machine that's so big you need steps to climb into it. On the front of the combine is a mechanism that does the hard work of harvesting the crops. The name, "combine," comes from the fact that the machine "combines" three different harvesting operations into one process: reaping, threshing, and winnowing (words you likely recognize from Scripture).

There was a palpable excitement in the air that Friday afternoon, the way that Eugene Peterson describes it in *The Message*: "When the grain is fully formed, he reaps—harvest time!"[1] This would be Scott's first weekend bringing in the harvest on his own, without his father calling the shots. His parents were headed out of town to a conference and wouldn't be home until Monday.

In the days leading up to their departure, Scott had been quietly calculating the number of acres he could harvest during the time his dad was away. While I dished up pot roast onto plates at supper, he would talk with high-pitched excitement to the girls, who were waiting in booster seats for their food. Would they want to go for a combine ride with him the next day? They shouted "Yes! Yes we do!" while banging little palms onto the pine table, then turned to me with pleading eyes: "Can we Mommy? *Can* we?" Scott envisioned shearing these fields, filling wagons with grain, and hauling them to the bins every night until the harvest moon slid up the night sky.

But that afternoon, it was obvious something wasn't right. Both Scott and his father heard a clanking sound deep inside the John Deere combine. An internal mechanism had broken, but they would need to empty the grain tank to discover what it was.

This, invariably, would delay the start of the harvest, which, for a farmer, is like telling a five-year-old boy his birthday has been postponed.

While always disappointing, mechanical breakdowns are a reality on the farm. Farmers are accustomed to such setbacks—well, *veteran* farmers are accustomed to them. Scott was still a rookie, not fully understanding the mechanics of complex equipment. This malfunction came with an added challenge: Scott would need to find the source of the problem on his own.

He thought his parents should cancel their trip, or at least delay it, but instead, his dad put his hands on his hips, shrugged, and said, "Sorry, son. We've gotta roll. Try to get it fixed."

Off he went.

And there Scott stood, on the perfect kind of harvesting day, with a gigantic problem waiting to be solved in the front yard. He not only felt unqualified for the task, he was pretty ticked.

He was mad at his dad. He was mad at the combine. He was mad at how this problem was messing up his plan for progress, on the first nice days of autumn. To borrow from the words of the prophet Joel, "Be dismayed, O farmers."[2] That fairly sums it up.

I don't know if Scott would have admitted it to you then, but beneath his anger, he was probably a bit scared.

What if he couldn't figure it out? What would it cost him? When time was of the essence, how far would this problem set back the harvest? What if he disappointed his dad?

Don't those sound like the questions we ask ourselves when things around us are breaking or falling apart?

Why now, God?

How can this be happening?

Can you fix this? Because I don't know how.

What will this cost—financially, emotionally, mentally, spiritually?

What if I disappoint my Father?

The combine malfunction created great frustration for Scott that year. However, there have been far more devastating things that have broken into pieces around our family—and likely around you. Some breakdowns have taken far too long to repair, and in some cases, broken pieces are still scattered at our feet.

Nothing is more disheartening than standing at the edge of your field, prepared to reap the rewards of hard work, only to have something break. This is the thing you're most afraid of: all of it breaking. You've spent months, even years, believing the seeds you planted in faith will bear much fruit in harvest. You've trusted God in the Growing Slow journey, taking one faithful step at a time, but you aren't seeing the yield that motivated you to keep taking the next step forward.

Our family is entering a certain kind of harvest this year. One daughter is now months away from graduating high school, and the other is trying to figure out the ups and downs of being a freshman in high school. There is so much joy in this season, the way a farmer feels when his crops are ready for harvest, but at the same time, it's been a hard season for us, filled with loss, disappointment, and grief. This is the paradox of life—the both/and of knowing that you hold joy in one hand and agony in the other. Recall once more the Ancient Way of Growing Slow—"For everything there is a season." Sometimes, two seasons happen simultaneously.

A friend told me she's observed how quickly people classify a year as good or bad. Often, she says, people are ready to leave one year behind and welcome a new one. In reality, each year has its ups and downs, and we'd all benefit from not classifying any given season, experience, or year as wholly good or wholly bad.

It is, indeed, possible to celebrate all that is good and beautiful during the golden harvest days, while at the same time reconciling the reality of all that has been upended by pain, health troubles, relational conflicts.

I am immensely grateful that I have a relationship with my daughters in which we talk and pray regularly about what they are facing—both blessing and blight. Because of this level of access to my daughters' interior lives, I know a lot about their struggles. But this access does not magically equip me to help my daughters, like I thought it would. Usually, I am acutely aware of my lack. This place of lack, I am learning, is not the worst place to be. Some of the most freeing words I've ever written were these from my book, *It's All Under Control*: "God hasn't given us the task of fixing everything."[3]

Yes, those are freeing words. They are also frightening.

Freeing, because when I say those words out loud, I'm reminding myself that God is working while we wait—his will, his timing, his way.

Frightening, because I don't like things to stay broken very long. I feel powerless around broken things. I am scared of broken things, and I fear what will happen if they don't get put back together again. I worry that God has flitted off to a conference, and because I am disposed to control issues, I try to tidy things up on my own.

When our daughters were younger, I could stand between them and their brokenness in some ways, shielding them through distraction, a night out at the movies, some ice cream, a longer tuck-in, and the promise that time would heal their wounds.

As the girls get older, it's harder to be a buffer between them and their heartache.

In Anna's health struggles, I have often felt powerless because I am unable to ease her emotional pain. When our older daughter, Lydia, deals with the trials of becoming an adult, I want to tie up every loose end and slap a happy bow on top of it all.

Not all of you are mothers. But even if you're not, you've planted seeds in other people—a spouse, an aging parent, the widow who sits next to you at book club. You've trusted that fruit would come.

Perhaps the brokenness you are experiencing isn't happening in the people around you, but within yourself as you cope with grief, doubt, apathy, feelings of uselessness, or uncertainty about God's plan for your life. Or, perhaps there's more: Betrayal. Disappointment. Rejection.

Few things feel more confusing or frustrating than finding yourself ankle deep in broken things. But the Ancient Way of Growing Slow means we embrace every season, even the seasons of breaking. There is a time for everything under the heavens, including "a time *to break down* and a time to build up."[4]

I don't want to be afraid of the breaking anymore. Instead, I want to lift every broken thing up to Jesus and say, "Can you fix this for us? Because we can't do this on our own. We can't farm on our own. We can't parent on our own. We can't hold these marriages together on our own. We can't do anything on our own. We trust you, Lord."

In this season of life, I see broken things all around me, like the world is cracking into a million unfixable little pieces. Marriages I thought would never fail are crumbling. Children who seemed sure-footed have lost their way as they enter adulthood. Addictions seize. Demons dwell. It's all too much.

Even inside myself, I feel how the brokenness of my past cuts into my present, making me feel ashamed, abandoned, and lonely.

But I don't want to be scared anymore. I want to believe that God is growing us through broken things, hard things, unknown things. That's just how he works. I wish there was another way, but again and again, this is how he does it.

I know it every time I turn my eyes to the cross, where brokenness healed all brokenness.

By his wounds you have been healed.[5]

My best efforts don't fix broken things. Only his brokenness does. My manipulation of circumstances won't fix broken things. Only his brokenness will. My frustration can't fix broken things. Only his brokenness can.

Jesus won't always take away the brokenness, but he will cover it with himself. He will cover it with his cross.

Brokenness isn't intended to break us. It's intended to *heal* us by leading us back to the cross. Brokenness leads us back to our need for Christ, our need for rescuing, and his ridiculously wonderful and unfathomable decision to save us all.

Oswald Chambers wrote that when we speak of the cross, the "energy of God is let loose."[6] I imagine that energy coming down to touch all the broken things, making them whole again.

All brokenness is simply a chance to let loose the energy of God on the cross—this energy that shook the earth and tore the veil and made the darkness hide. Our brokenness is an opportunity to be healed and made whole by Jesus—to lift up our broken pieces of life to a God who sees us and whispers, "I can do something with this. I already have."

God, who led you to your fields, was with you when you planted those first seeds. He sits next to you when you weep over loss, and he rejoices with you when you are bringing in the sheaves.

That autumn weekend on the farm, Scott figured out how to drain the tank of harvested soybeans and find the broken part deep inside the combine. He called a guy at a repair shop, ordered a part, and the next day, the two of them worked together to replace the broken part on one of the grain augers.

For the rest of the harvest, Scott kept looking back on that weekend as utterly wasted.

But not anymore. Just yesterday, Scott told me he believes that weekend was a kind of gift. His dad, who was a schoolteacher before he was a farmer, had a teacher's heart. And he knew that some lessons are best learned in the midst of brokenness.

More than anything, Scott's dad wanted to teach his son how to be a farmer—how to run the equipment, buy and sell at the right times, watch the markets, care for sick pigs, and all the other things that farmers do. There were so many lessons but too little time.

A few months before he passed away, as the cancer raged in his failing body, the father said to the son, "There's so much I haven't taught you."

The lesson Scott remembers most often is the one that unfolded on the driveway that day. Last autumn, Scott had the same problem with his combine again. This time, he knew exactly what to do.

The very thing that distressed my husband became the thing that grew him.

Could it be that the brokenness in your own life is the pathway to growth?

Dear brothers and sisters, when troubles of any kind come your way, consider it an opportunity for great joy. For you know that when your faith is tested, your endurance has a chance to grow. So let it grow.[7]

So let it grow.

Broken things are fertilizer for the growth you'll see in a new season.

Broken things are sometimes the most beautiful things of all. So break your will. Break your plans. Take the bottle of alabaster in your hand, and smash it into a thousand pieces at the feet of Jesus. Know that your broken offering of love is seen by the One who makes you whole.

And he will. He will make you whole. He will bring you to the harvest. It's his plan. It's his promise.

So let it grow.

REMEMBER

God grows us through broken things.

REFLECT

Think of a time when the harvest seemed within reach, but all your hopes were dashed. Reread the questions on page 149. Did you ask any of those kinds of questions when your hopes for a bountiful harvest were dashed?

....

....

....

....

....

In her book *The Broken Way*, Ann Voskamp writes, "All of us in a heartbreaking world, we are the fellowship of the broken . . . Over all of us is the image of the wounded God, the God who breaks open and bleeds with us. *How do you live with your one broken heart?* All I can think is—only the wounds of God can heal our wounds."[8] How does this communion with God—where suffering is healed by suffering—intersect with your brokenness today?

....

....

....

....

....

RETURN

At the end of each chapter,
we return to the soil.

Our God, who does not lie, tells us that "at the proper time
we will reap a harvest if we do not give up."[9] Write a prayer
here thanking God in advance for the harvest to come.

CHAPTER 15

THE BLEACHER PEOPLE

G rowing up, I was a proud member of the Poland Ever Energetic 4-H Club. The club was open to any young female living in Poland Township, no matter if you were a town girl or a farm girl. The boys had their own club: the Poland Plowboys.

Whether boy or girl, we all solemnly pledged our heads to clearer thinking, our hearts to greater loyalty, our hands to larger service, our health to better living—for our club, our community, our country, and our world. (Yes, the 4-H pledge burns into one's memory.)

The crowning moment for any 4-H member was the annual county fair, where—if you were a country kid—you would lead your cow, sheep, pig, or goat around the show ring with the hope of bringing home a blue ribbon. I was a town kid, but I looked forward to the fair just the same. I would bring what were called "static exhibits" for evaluation before a panel of judges. I still remember my blue-ribbon-winning photo of a sunset, my no-bake brownies arranged meticulously on a paper plate, and a carefully constructed cross-stitch project of two cuddly bears.

So years later, when our daughters announced that they wanted to join the Country Kids 4-H Club here, I was so tickled. It felt like time was folding over on itself.

It's a new era for 4-H, and our daughters' club was for boys and girls. That first year, I attended most of the meetings, some held outdoors on the front porch of a friend's farmhouse. A boy—still getting used to his deepening voice—called the meeting to order with the help of a gavel. We all stood to recite the 4-H pledge and the Pledge of Allegiance, while a tiny flag flapped on a wooden stick in the breeze. The 4-H leader called for nominations for club officers, and Lydia stood up tall, nominating herself for the position of 4-H reporter. The winner would be responsible for writing news stories about the meetings for the local weekly. Lydia won.

Like Lydia, I had been the reporter. And just like when I was a kid, Lydia looked forward to the county fair. Over the years, we hauled sheep (Kayla and Peanut), pigs (Digger, Fat Albert, and Bacon), and calves (Sherbet and Daisy) to the fair in hopes of blue-ribbon performances.

During one of our first years at the county fair, we unloaded the calves from the trailer and bedded them down in their pens. The sweet scent of hay, mixed with the not-so-subtle whiff of manure, transported me back to my earliest fairs as a child. Honestly, I never imagined I'd have children who would show livestock for sport. Being inexperienced with livestock—remember, I was a town kid—I felt clumsy and incompetent trying to figure out how to open the gates, clean the animals' stalls, and cajole jumpy calves into heading toward the show ring.

One afternoon, I was sitting on the bleachers that surround the show ring. The bucket calf show had begun, and Lydia was about to present her calf, Sherbet. Sitting there, I had a sudden awareness that I was not like the other farm moms around me. They knew how to tie knots in ropes, how to lock the gates behind them, and how to wear the appropriate footwear, for heaven's sake. Many of them were wearing work boots, or at least closed-toe tennis shoes. Me? I had on cute flip-flops bejeweled with fake rhinestones. My lips were lined in bougainvillea red. I looked down at my hands and realized I had foolishly gotten my nails manicured the week before the county fair. (It was a holdover habit from my days in the news business.)

It hit me like a surprise: I did not fit in. I don't know how I missed it, *but I had definitely missed it*. I'm sure I was the last person in the tri-county area to realize what everyone else had known for months: I was . . . *different*.

Just then, a farmer—the husband of a woman I'd recently befriended—walked over to where I sat on the bleachers. His words cut deep and sealed the deal: "You're like a fish out of water, aren't you?" he said. He laughed and walked away.

My heart sank. I was embarrassed. In time, I made the deliberate choice to believe that the man meant no harm; he merely observed and stated the obvious. It was true. I *was* a fish out of water. I didn't have the abilities or fashion tastes of a farm wife, whatever one was "supposed to" be like. People didn't know me as "Jennifer," but as "Scott's wife." So yeah, fish out of water was maybe a little accurate.

You can't forget a thing like that.

You can't always forget the way that people look at you, the words they speak over you, or the way they evaluate you.

I'll bet you know what I mean.

There will always be people in our bleachers.

Yes, we all have metaphorical bleachers, and there are people sitting upon them, spectators of your life.

Like it or not, you have an audience. It includes kind and loving people. These people cheer you on as you head toward the finish line, even when you are out of place with your bejeweled flip-flops. Among them are wise and discerning voices who have invested time and energy in your life, and you in theirs. You might not like everything you hear from them, but they've earned the right to speak truth to you.

But there are other Bleacher People, unhelpful critics who seem to habitually misunderstand you, doubt you, test you, or passive-aggressively critique you. You may have known some of these Bleacher People for a long time. They are familiar with the most tender places in your heart and your vulnerabilities, and because of that, they know where to hurt you most. The Bleacher People also include strangers who somehow think they've earned the right to evaluate the life you're building.

My bleachers are scattered with people in all of the above categories. I've grown used to being a little bit outside of what people expect me to be as a farm wife, and I have—for the most part—been accepted for who I am. I hope I have done the same to others. Most people are really good people. I believe that with all my heart.

But one of the weird ways Bleacher People show up in my life these days is through book reviews. Many of my author friends tell me I shouldn't read reviews, but I do. I read the ones that tell me how a book I wrote switched something in their soul, gave them hope, and led them to a new outlook on life.

I also read the ones that tell me I'm a terrible writer. One such Amazon reviewer said my writing was "very shallow and tedious" and gave one of my books two stars. Later, the same reviewer gave her favorite mascara a five-star rating and called it a "life-saver." Who am I to stand between a girl and her favorite mascara?

A friend recently asked me how I deal with criticism. I told her I deal with critics the same way I deal with praise: I remember that I am not the sum of what anyone says about me, good or bad. So you can say nice things about me, and it will make me smile, but your praise is not who I am. Or you can say bad things about me, and it might sting a little, but that's not who I am, either.

Some time ago, I committed a quote by Amy Carmichael to memory: "If the praise of man elates me and his blame depresses me; if I cannot rest under misunderstanding without defending myself; if I love to be loved more than to love . . . then I know nothing of Calvary love."[1]

You are not the sum of the great things the Bleacher People say to you, or the bad press they spread about you. You can't make everyone happy; you are not five-star mascara. And your life is not under the jurisdiction of a committee.

The truth is, not everyone will appreciate what you are up to in this life of yours. Not everyone will "get" what you've been growing in your fields. They may question your priorities and preferences.

If that's you, then you are in good company, friend. Jesus understands.

His life was filled with Bleacher People. They were constantly questioning him, criticizing him, and testing him. His actions were often misunderstood, and the words he spoke were regularly taken out of context. Under direct criticism, Jesus messed with people a little bit. He intentionally healed people on the Sabbath, which he certainly knew would send religious leaders into a rage.

Even Jesus' own family struggled to understand his behavior and decisions at times. "They went to take charge of him, for they said, 'He is out of his mind.'"[2]

At one point, Jesus went back to his hometown. If any of your Bleacher People are going to cheer for you, it would be the ones who grew up with you, right? That's not how it worked for Jesus. He went home, taking along his disciples, and began to teach. But the people in his childhood community "took offense at him."[3]

Haters gonna hate, but Jesus gonna love.

Jesus mostly blew off the Bleacher People instead of fighting them. In fact, he taught people to pray for their enemies, one of the highest forms of love. Jesus moved from village to village to heal, teach, befriend, and do the work God called him to do: the spiritual harvesting of souls.

He stayed focused on his purpose.

> When they hurled insults at him, he did not retaliate; when he suffered, he made no threats. Instead, he entrusted himself to him who judges justly.[4]

I don't know about you, but my heart gets especially hurried when I think I've got to hustle to impress people in the bleachers. One way to un-hurry your heart is to come to terms with the fact that not everyone will like you.

There will always be critics.

Don't let them stop you. Don't stop making your art. Don't stop writing your book. Don't muzzle your voice, or consign your paint brushes, or bury your dreams in the cemetery of good intentions because people don't get what you're growing in those fields. Some people will make you think you're doing too much; others will accuse you of doing too little.

Not everyone will understand what you're growing, but that doesn't mean what you're growing isn't important.

It's time for us to clear the bleachers. You and I were made for a very small audience: an audience of One. Jesus is your #1 Bleacher Person.

This doesn't mean we stop listening to constructive criticism from the voices of people who are invested in our lives; some of the criticism will change us for the better. But it does mean that we stop letting everyone else have the loudest voice in our lives.

Paul wrote, "It matters very little how I might be evaluated by you or by any human authority."[5]

He cleared the bleachers. We can do the same.

What would that look like for you? How would clearing the bleachers settle your hurried heart?

Here's how it works for me. My life is somewhat public as a writer and speaker. I stand in front of literal audiences at conferences sometimes.

It takes a lot for me to step onto the stage because of my fear of public speaking. But I have learned that my fear is closely linked to pride. I have long wanted the people in the seats to like me. In order to be an effective servant at these events, I've had to let go of the fear of doing it wrong.

So whenever I take the stage these days, I remind myself that the goal isn't for someone to like me or think I'm funny or wise. My job isn't to tell a good story. My job is simply to point to Jesus. I don't speak so that the people in the room will fall more in love with me. I speak so that by the time I'm finished, the people in the room will leave more in love with Jesus than when they showed up.

Jesus left a legacy of perfectly loving his Father and living only for an audience of One.

We can do the same thing.

When we get to heaven, our heavenly Father will be waiting for us. What will he tell us "well done" for?

He won't want to talk about our earthly approval ratings, our striving, our accomplishments, or anything like that.

He will say "well done" for taking what he gave us—these fields and these seeds—and using them all for his glory, for his applause alone.

The greatest reward of the harvest will come from the words of your Father:

"Well done, good and faithful servant! . . . Come and share your master's happiness!"[6]

REMEMBER

Not everyone will understand what
you're growing, but that doesn't mean
what you're growing isn't important.

REFLECT

Take a moment to think about the people who sit in your
bleachers. How have your Bleacher People encouraged
you?

How have they belittled you?

How can seeking the approval of Bleacher People cause
us to have hurried hearts?

Name an area where you most need to remember that
you live for an audience of One.

RETURN

At the end of each chapter,
we return to the soil.

There's an old hymn that tells us what type of ground to set our feet upon.

> On Christ, the solid, Rock, I stand;
> All other ground is sinking sand.

Rock isn't a great place to grow a seed. But it's a great place to put your feet when you clear the bleachers. If there's someone who's been sitting in your bleachers for far too long, now would be a great time to pray for God's voice to drown out the voice of the unhelpful spectator.

PART 4

WINTER REST

In seed time learn, in harvest teach, in winter enjoy.

WILLIAM BLAKE

CHAPTER 16

HOW TO GROW IN THE DARK

A nd then comes winter.

I don't know a single person who describes herself as a "winter person."

Everything feels harder in winter: getting out of bed, driving, eating healthy, motivating myself to accomplish something, washing my hair, changing out of pajamas.

Going to the grocery store on a subzero winter day in the Midwest is like dressing for a hike up Everest—hat drawn over the ears, scarf pulled up to your eyeballs, musty parka, thick gloves. In winter, my neighbors post memes on social media that say things like, "Why do I live where the air hurts my face?" We're constantly battling snot, wind-reddened cheeks, icy windshields, winter storm warnings, and darkness.

Oh, the darkness.

I realize I'm starting to sound like our grandparents, who claimed to have walked miles to school, uphill, both ways.

No matter where you live, it's likely winter isn't your favorite season. In fact, one poll of Americans showed that fewer than 10 percent liked winter the most.[1] Winter can feel pointless, empty, barren, and devoid of light.

Spring is celebrated for its perennial hope. Summer, for its warmth and brightness, long days, and firefly nights. Autumn, for its blazing beauty and its harvests.

Then comes winter with its icy fingers. It can feel like an assault on our bodies and our psyches. Yet winter is part of the natural progression of seasons on Earth and seasons of the heart. The Ancient Way reminds us that there is a season for every activity under heaven—even winter.

When I was a child, I embraced winter. The first snow always felt magical, holding the promise of snowmen, forts, new Moon Boots, thick socks, and hot chocolate. My little brother and I would slip on snowsuits and run outside through the evergreen trees, working up a sweat even on the coldest days. On weekends, we would head to the woods and zoom down the hills on inner tubes Dad had inflated in the garage back home.

Winter was a season of magic. What if we could embrace winter like a child again?

There is a hidden gift in winter, tucked away in secret for those of us who have adopted a Growing Slow mindset. We might think that because it's winter, nothing is growing at all. But that's not true; winter is the season when we might experience the best growth of all: growth in character, in rest, in dependence, in trust, and in the art of celebrating the work of planting and harvest.

When we adopt the pace of winter, we turn inward and take time to reflect. Winter validates the melancholy part of us, reminding us it's okay to sit in the dark and be sad sometimes. By enforcing semi-hibernation, winter gives us permission to embrace the quiet, to turn away from distractions and busyness, to find cozy corners in long-neglected places, and then to simply just *be*.

Let me be honest, though: on the coldest days of winter, it's hard for me to embrace the season like a child.

Winter on our farm isn't the sort of thing you'd see gracing the cover of *Country Living* magazine. When winter storms strike, the removal of snow from our driveway and farm entrances can take many hours, even a whole day. At least once every winter, we are literally snowed in, while our country roads are iced over or under the perilous assault of blowing snow. Winter is definitely not all picturesque, with a roaring fire and hot cocoa in hand. On some of those blisteringly cold days, it's downright miserable. I'll hear Scott muttering out in the garage as he stomps the snow off his boots. I won't lie about it: my gentle-hearted husband could cuss the hind end off a hog on a wind-whipping winter day.

But even on the regular days, winter can feel dreary and boring, even a bit pointless, as the fields hibernate. It's the same schedule every day: the pigs need to be fed and watered. Farm equipment needs to be checked and fixed. And there are piles of paperwork to be completed.

By February, our addiction to productivity is an itch that begs to be scratched.

But in my Growing Slow journey, I began to sense something: I have missed the hidden gift of winter.

Perhaps winter is meant to be restorative for us, but if so, do we truly receive this gift?

Many of us avoid winter. Often, Scott and I have flown out of here for a weeklong respite on a faraway beach. Some people leave for much longer. In the Upper Midwest, retired people— called snowbirds—seasonally migrate for a few months of escape in Arizona or Florida.

We are always itching to escape winter. But what if winter isn't a season to be escaped, and instead, one to be embraced?

In past centuries, escape wasn't a possibility. Because of a lack of transportation and electricity, winter literally slowed people down, as they gathered in their homes around burning logs in the fireplace, lanterns, oil lamps, and candles. Today, the uncomfortable seasons of our natural world can become practically irrelevant. If it's dark outside, we flip a switch for artificial light. If it's cold, we push a button on the digital thermostat. We carry on with our busy lives, drawing the shades on winter and trudging forward—always trudging forward.

Let's open the shades and see the hidden gifts of winter.

Winter Seasons of the Heart

One way we cope with winter is by reminding ourselves that the season will eventually make way for spring. To be sure, the harshness of winter makes spring that much sweeter.

But what if winter is more than a season to be tolerated until we arrive somewhere better? What if winter is more than a required passageway to reach the prize of spring?

Winter is not just a doorway; it is a room all its own, with treasures to be discovered and pondered.

Looking back, I can see that the winter seasons of my life grew me in ways I didn't know I needed at the time. They grew faith inside of me that I never imagined possible. In my heart's coldest winters, I learned about perseverance, patience, and endurance, traits that would serve me well in the summers of my heart.

During the winter seasons of life, it appeared as though nothing was happening, and that nothing I did mattered.

There were years of exhaustion, seasons of loneliness, long hospital stays, emergencies, funerals, financial strain, disappointments in ministry, and so much more. I struggled with a dark night of the soul during a long stretch of my early adulthood. In those years, I lost all belief, not only in Jesus' love for me, but in his very existence.

I am certain your list of wintry trials is lengthy as well.

Scripture makes it clear: Christians don't get a pass on hard times. Such moments must be endured. Even so, I would beg God to end the winter seasons of my heart, to bring springtime to my soul.

Immediate relief did not always come. During one winter season of my heart, in 2004, my oldest sister, Juliann, gave me a piece of paper on which she had written the words, "Give me enough grace for today."

God didn't always move the mountain, but day by day, he provided me with enough grace to climb it. Strength for today; hope for tomorrow. Each day, I added to the muscle and spiritual insight that I would not have gained any other way.

Winter seasons of the heart can reveal themselves not only in times of great trial but in the mundane moments of life—these moments on the farm when the days feel long and boring, when the tractors are in hibernation.

As a mom of young children, I sometimes wondered, *What if this is as good as it gets?* What if my ordinary life—returning library books, folding clothes, running errands, doing life with the same people, eating the same Crock-Pot meals on rotation—is as good as it gets? What if the tangled mess of muddy shoes at the back door is as good as it gets? What if the fingerprints on the windows are as good as it gets? What if the size of my waist is the smallest it will ever be, despite my best efforts? What if the bank account has already reached its largest sum ever, and it's all downhill from here?

What if this is all as good as it gets? Because it might be true. This could be as good as it gets, and it also could be more spectacular than I ever realized.

Now that I've been intentionally moving through this Growing Slow journey, I see it. I see in hindsight what I couldn't see in real time: The fingerprints, shoes, laundry, my quirky bunch of friends, my flawed family, my skin, the just-enough grace for every single day—together, they become the sum of a beautiful story that stretches across my little time in history, on my little patch of land. All those moments, though seemingly small at the time, were building a foundation for who I would become.

Maybe these winter moments of life are "as good as it gets," and if we look a little closer, it's not only "as good as it gets," it's greater than we knew. Everything that looks mundane and difficult and boring and regular and barren is actually holy and sacred, gilded with the grace of God and "thy kingdom come."

We could be so eager for some other season to arrive that we miss the ordinary miracle of this moment, right now.

As we un-hurry our hearts, let's not rush through the seasons. Let's grow slow here. Let's see the winter not as something that must be endured, but something that must be treasured. God will use winter seasons to grow us.

The land teaches us the truth of the winter blessing.

My husband tells me that in order for the soil to be ready for spring, it needs the cold, dark months of winter. Here's why.

Frost, snow, and cold temperatures all serve to prepare the land for the coming spring. Frost disrupts pest and disease cycles, and it actually improves the soil. Around here, snow is called "poor man's fertilizer." As snow falls, it picks up nitrogen on the way down. When the snow thaws, it slowly melts, quietly releasing nitrogen into the soil. We think that because it's winter, nothing is happening in the fields. But that's not true at all. There is a lot of work going on in the dark, below the surface, that will greatly impact the growth of the coming year.

There is so much that happens in the dark, even now, in places you can't see. The land is alive, breathing, preparing itself for the season to come.

The same is true of us.

We are alive, breathing, being prepared for the season to come.

When I began outlining the chapters of this book, I almost talked myself out of ending the book with winter, because the face of winter looks bleak and dark. But after writing this book and living the message of Growing Slow, I am more convinced than ever that it makes sense to finish strong in the places that might look hopeless to you right now. In winter.

In the chapters ahead, we will explore healing, rest, celebration, restoration, and legacy. We will reflect on our fields and be grateful for the rhythms built into creation. We will let the seasons take their course—even in us. We will find him—and his love and grace—even on the darkest night.

Spring will come. But it can wait. Let's not rush to get there. A little winter in your heart beckons you to stay, to ponder, to savor.

Come, let us grow slow.

REMEMBER

Winter is not just a doorway;
it is a room all its own.

REFLECT

Few people describe themselves as a "winter person."
Would you? Why or why not?

....

....

....

....

What lessons have you learned in the winter seasons of
your life?

....

....

....

....

....

What gifts come with winter?

....

....

....

....

....

RETURN

*At the end of each chapter,
we return to the soil.*

How do you suppose "poor man's fertilizer" (page 174) is preparing your own soil?

....
....
....
....
....
....
....
....
....
....
....
....
....
....
....
....
....
....
....
....
....
....
....
....
....

CHAPTER 17

THE SLOW, HEALING
WORK OF GOD

In my corner of the world, there's at least one nasty ice storm every winter, the kind that can turn a parking lot into a glistening skating rink in minutes. Iced-over trees droop headfirst toward the ground, audibly groaning under the weight. Ice so thoroughly covers everyone's windows that my neighbor calls the effect "cheap blinds."

Ice storms represent the worst part of winter. It's easy to think that once winter comes, all is lifeless and harsh on the other side of the cheap blinds. But make no mistake: the land is very much alive during winter, doing hidden, meaningful work that prepares the earth—and everything in her—for spring.

I probably learned that fascinating biological fact in a high school science class many years ago, but I didn't pay attention to its truth until I lived on a farm. I know it now: there is so much happening underneath the soil during winter, vital functions shielded entirely from our sight. The part that astounds me most is how the earth uses the bone-chilling misery of ice as a power source to propel rocks to the surface—rocks that were invisible and buried only a few months earlier. Here's a little science lesson: Over the winter, water under the soil freezes, and when it does, it also expands, pushing unseen rocks upward. The freeze/thaw cycle will eventually produce enough force to heave buried stones forth. It's a miracle, really, that a solid lump can be pushed, against the forces of gravity, to find its way toward the light. This is the labor and delivery of Mother Earth.

It turns out Mother Earth can birth some pretty big babies.

Recently, Scott texted me from our field down by the river. "Would you look at this?" he wrote. I opened the image to see a jagged rock the approximate size of our living room recliner. Scott had to use a skid loader to dig it out and haul it away.

Any farmer will tell you rocks that surface in fields are a nuisance, but they simply must be dealt with. If they are left in the fields, even fist-sized stones can harm the farming equipment during cultivating, planting, and harvest.

Let's "Pick Rock"

As a preteen girl growing up in the rural Midwest, my first job wasn't "waitress" or "lifeguard." It was "rock picker."

The work was about as glamorous as it sounds.

A local farmer—usually my best friend's dad, Carl, or my godfather, Gaylon—would drive through the neighborhood in a pickup truck and round up a bunch of kids to come out to the farm and "pick rock." It was a funny phrase, now that I think of it, because we didn't pick just one rock. There were hundreds, even thousands.

A parent would drive a bunch of us out to the farm, and we'd seat ourselves on a flatbed trailer or hayrack. Our feet would dangle over the edge, and off we went. The farmer would drive his tractor straight into the field, pulling us behind on the trailer as we jostled with every bump. Our job was to keep our eyes open for rocks. If you saw a rock, you hopped off the trailer, ran to grab it, and hollered "Rock!" before tossing it onto the trailer. The shout was a sort of warning, so the others would hop off or move out of the way to avoid being clobbered in the head. (Clearly, we had high workplace safety standards.) Our little team of rock pickers covered miles a day in search of stones.

The next year, we'd be picking rock in the very same fields, because new ones always emerged. The labor and delivery of Mother Earth is never-ending.

In unglamorous winter—when the land is quiet, the days short, and the nights unbearably long—something remarkable is happening in invisible places. Hibernating animals are sleeping, while their tiny chests rise and fall. Microbes are active, working mysteriously in a way that is crucial for growing a healthy food supply. Rocks are moving.

Scott calls the process "a healing of the land." In this healing, rocks emerge.

Also, trees and plants go dormant. It's a natural reset, and without it, these precious living things wouldn't survive.

If a tree needs to take a break, why do we think we should keep running on all cylinders? If the stillness of winter works a kind of magic to heal the land, why do we think we have to keep running all the time?

What if we need winter, too?

These questions invigorate me, enlivening the part of me that has previously disdained winter as an annoyance that stood between me and my progress.

Practically speaking, I haven't wintered well. My inclination is not to slow down, unless I'm forced. My eyes habitually scan the horizon for next steps and further instructions, and I feel the itch to keep going, keep growing, without stopping to catch my breath.

But what this Growing Slow journey has taught me is this: Winter is not a season of death. It is a season of life, way-down-in-the-depth-of-it-all life. Winter is alive and, dare I say, essential—not only to the land, but to us.

I know winter looks un-spectacular, even meaningless. There are no seeds to sow, no fields to fill, no harvest to haul. Few would actively choose to live through seasons of hibernation, especially when you look around and observe the hustle culture on full display in spectacular ways that look like success. Even if it's only an illusion, you see every other woman in the world winning, living in a constant cycle of plant-grow-harvest, plant-grow-harvest. With her tanned and toned arms and her sun-kissed cheeks, she is killin' it at every level, and completely leapfrogging over winter. She is fit, funny, wildly successful, and universally loved.

And me? I'm living my best life, eating Doritos straight from the bag while sitting cross-legged on the pantry floor in an oversized sweatshirt and drawstring joggers that haven't been washed for three days.

I think we need to reframe winter seasons, because there's little doubt that we are all going to face them. It's not always our turn or our moment to shine.

Sometimes, there will be nothing spectacular happening in our fields, and we will have to sit it out. Winter will tell us, "Today, there is nothing to do or produce." Sometimes, our only task is to nourish our rest-starved selves with simple, un-hurried acts of soul-keeping: slow walks, slow food, soft music, flickering candles, and simply being present with Jesus.

That's what winter is for.

For a culture that really likes "doing" and "achieving," *slow* can be a hard word to hear. But perhaps, like a tree, we won't survive without winter. This is a season for our healing—thanks be to God—in the same way that the coldest night beneath the aurora borealis can push forth a rock by morning.

The Ancient Way of Growing Slow reminds us that there is a

time for every matter under heaven, every happy thing and every hard thing, every chuckle and every tear, and every season known to man.

The Ancient Way makes space for ancient stones to rise up and break through the soil, and we must go out into the fields to gather them.

There is a time for everything, . . .
A time to scatter stones and *a time to gather them.*[1]

The Stones Within

I have carried stones, long buried in my soul. Stones are the unseen burdens I haul around in my heart like unwanted baggage, picked up along the way of life.

My stones are heavy and jagged and ugly:

Hurtful words spoken over me when I was a child.
Deep-seated beliefs that I'll never really be enough.
The secret fear that I'm not lovable.
Past sins I drag around with me because I don't fully accept
    forgiveness or believe I'm worthy.
New, bad habits I pick up over time.
Coping mechanisms that numb me to pain.
A long history of unbelief and distrust that affects my
    relationship with God and with people.

These are my stones. They are not pretty.

I am good at keeping old stones buried. It's easy: I'll keep the hand to the plow and simply take a pass on winter, thank you very much, so I don't have to contend with hidden stones and past hurts.

But hidden stones still cut your insides, a slow slaying of the soul.

Get a little quiet now and hear your soul pleading with you: "Let winter do its work."

You've read enough of my story in this book to know that I am not the poster child of rest, but I can now testify to its good work. In my Growing Slow journey, I found winter to be a trustworthy school of soul-keeping. Sometimes, I hope the teacher is grading on the curve, because I'm not a model student. But I'm learning a lot about myself. I'm learning who I am as a daughter of God— not as a consumer or a producer or a grower. Winter does, indeed, heal. It reveals what hurts my soul: toxic people, long-held beliefs that I'm not any good, my fear of falling behind, my hurried heart, and my nose-to-the-grindstone personality. It also has unearthed stones, buried for so many years, that are still being hauled away. New cycles of winter will unearth new rocks, just like on the farm.

Winter also reveals what makes a soul grow: meaningful, eye-to-eye connection; deep conversation; an awareness of God's presence in my everyday life; work that is consequential and sustainable but that doesn't annihilate me in the process.

True winter rest is more than a nap or a day at the spa. It's more than a recharge for tomorrow's work. It's deep and necessary soul tending.

We have all observed what happens when people never hop off the hamster wheel. They keep driving, keep grinding, keep plodding:

Plant another church.
Maximize more growth.
Build another empire.
Attract a few more followers.
Live up to the expectations of the boss, the board, the
    congregation, the parents.
Grow, grow, and grow some more!

I know many people who rarely take vacations—that is, until they get so stressed out and sick that they have no choice but to take a break. One study showed that more than half of Americans leave their paid vacation days on the table.[2] If people *do* decide to take a vacation, they work overtime to cram in a bunch of work before they activate their out-of-office email message.

Alison Green writes, "Too often, employees are made to feel like there's no good time for them to get away. They worry that they can't leave because there's no one to cover their work or that projects will pile up, requiring too much work and stress to catch up once they're back."[3]

Better is a handful of quietness than two hands full of toil and a striving after wind.[4]

God did not call us to this life of burnout. He called us to a set aside time for rest, healing, and sabbath. Even the land itself was given a God-ordained break; every seventh year, the land was to lie fallow.[5]

If I want to produce good fruit, I must let my field lie fallow a while.

Tuck inside.

Rest.

Heal.

Take a break and call out the value of tenderness, quietness, and slowness. Stop idolizing doggedness and multitasking.

Lord Jesus, save me from myself. Help me to sit down and get cozy in winter. Deliver me from my unending series of yeses to everyone and everything. Deliver me from the fear that I am falling behind and from the misguided notion that you created people to be perpetually in motion.

God is going to call us to do a lot of wonderful things in this

life, but he will not call us to a life of burnout. He didn't breathe
air into the lungs of a machine; he breathed air into flesh and
blood. Humans get tired, have eyelids that close, have muscles that
weaken, have feet that ache, have brains that need quieting. And it's
okay—necessary, even—to replenish your inner resources.

You may worry that stepping away from it all is going to kill
your progress, but what if it's the thing that saves your ministry,
your family, your business?

Perhaps winter isn't the punishment you thought it was. Perhaps
it is a gift.

What if this is the winter you decide to go fallow? Even if winter
feels forced on you by circumstances out of your control, what if
you embrace it as quiet space for your healing? What loss still needs
to be mourned? What past hurt needs to be reckoned with? What
muscle needs rest? What rocks need to be hauled away?

Trust in the Slow Work of God

Pierre Teilhard de Chardin knew a thing or two about rocks and
rest. He was both a theologian and a geologist. Let the words of his
classic, poetic prayer, "Trust in the Slow Work of God," find a soft
place in your heart today.

> Above all, trust in the slow work of God.
> We are quite naturally impatient in everything
> to reach the end without delay.
> We should like to skip the intermediate stages.
> We are impatient of being on the way to something
>   unknown, something new.
> And yet it is the law of all progress
> that it is made by passing through some stages of
>   instability—

and that it may take a very long time.
And so I think it is with you.
Your ideas mature gradually—let them grow,
let them shape themselves, without undue haste.
Don't try to force them on,
as though you could be today what time
(that is to say, grace and circumstances acting on your
    own good will)
will make of you tomorrow.
Only God could say what this new spirit
gradually forming within you will be.
Give Our Lord the benefit of believing
that his hand is leading you,
and accept the anxiety of feeling yourself
in suspense and incomplete.[6]

Let's scrape the ice off the windows and behold the gift of winter. "Give Our Lord the benefit of believing that his hand is leading you."
Even here.
Even now.
Someday, it will be your turn. Someday, it will be your moment to shine. Someday, the harvest will be meant just for you.
Right here in winter, I hope you find it is worth waiting for.

REMEMBER

Perhaps winter isn't the punishment you thought it was. Perhaps it is your gift.

REFLECT

Think of a time when it was clear it wasn't your turn, but someone else's. How did that sit with you?

....

....

....

Pierre Teilhard de Chardin contends that we like to skip intermediate stages and get to the end without delay. How have you found that to be true in your own life?

....

....

....

Trees need dormant seasons in order to survive and thrive. Name a time in your life when winter dormancy brought a better and brighter bloom, come spring.

....

....

....

....

RETURN

At the end of each chapter, we return to the soil.

On page 183, I shared about some of the stones, long-buried, in the soil of my heart. What are the stones in your field? Let winter do its work by unearthing those stones. Let's "pick rock." Write down your "stones" here.

CHAPTER 18

THE FIVE THINGS WE CAN'T AFFORD TO FORGET

When I began writing the first chapters of this book, I thought a Growing Slow mindset was mostly a matter of will. With God's help, and enough determination, we would hop off the hamster wheel in search of a quieter, slower, more mindful existence. I stand by the belief that Growing Slow takes daily intentionality. There's little doubt that un-hurrying our hearts will require the breaking down of old habits and the building up of new and sustainable ones.

That's always how it works, right? Countering the psychology of speed demands a conscious rebellion. Slowing down doesn't just happen.

Until, it does "just happen."

Because that's exactly what happened to all of us, everywhere around the world.

A Growing Slow mindset was forced upon humanity.

At times, it felt like a strange dream, and at other times, like a horrible nightmare. It was the pandemic of the century, caused by COVID-19.

I am writing this chapter in the very early stages of this world-wide pandemic and resulting lockdown. I am isolated with my family from the outside world. My thoughts are fresh and raw, and part of me knows that by the time this book reaches your hands, my preliminary reflections could feel outdated and immature. Yet I will write them anyway. I can't help but think that what we experienced in the early days of the pandemic has something to teach us in later seasons of life. I think it's important that we recount how we lived these moments in real time, before we saw the breakthrough, before we saw a silver lining or the healing. It's important to remember where we saw God in our midst, even as our comforts were stripped away.

Do you remember where you were when the virus became a reality for you? Perhaps it was the moment you read the email from the school superintendent informing you school was canceled until further notice. Or maybe it was when your hairdresser called to cancel your appointment, and weeks later you made the mistake of coloring your own roots. Or perhaps it was that growing irritation you felt every time you went to the store to find toilet paper that was never there.

As days turned to weeks, the tragedy deepened, affecting nearly every corner of our lives: the economy, our workplaces and schools, our freedom to move about, our health, and the lives of those we loved who fell ill.

I do not want to dismiss the abject heartbreak and tremendous tragedy. We've paid a hefty price.

Yet I want us to pause and think back to what we learned in those early days. I remember pawing through the rubble of the novel coronavirus to pluck strange gifts, shining like diamonds. We were given the opportunity—previously inconceivable—to see what it would look like if the world stopped. The bluest, clearest skies appeared over Delhi, because pollution halted. Coyotes walked the empty roads of San Francisco, while peacocks picked their way along stranded streets in Ronda, Spain. Colorful seashells piled up on beaches because there were no tourists to carry them away. People in cities asked why the birds were louder. They weren't louder; people could just hear them better because everything else was so much quieter. It was both ethereal and eerie. And it was worldwide, a fact that carried with it a quiet call to solidarity among us all.

There were obvious exceptions to the slowdown, of course. Not everyone could fully press pause. I know many young moms who said they were busier than ever. We have farm friends in Illinois who modified their whiskey distillery operation so they could crank out thousands of gallons of corn-based hand sanitizer. They could hardly find time to sleep because they were also suddenly trying to shepherd their kids through online learning.

Also? I hope, by now, that every doctor, nurse, pharmacist, and grocery store clerk around the world has been given some kind of medal for bravery.

For many of us, the treadmills we'd been running on suddenly stopped. The fall from our hurried life hurt, to be sure. But when we stood up and brushed ourselves off, we found that scales had fallen from our eyes.

For my family, it meant that we were all at the table for every single meal, with no expectation to be anywhere but present with each other. It meant long walks every evening along country roads. I saw parts of my little world—only a mile away—that I had never previously inspected! It also meant self-quarantining so I could feel safe delivering groceries to my elderly parents without fear of infecting them. It meant contemplating hard decisions about school, high school graduation, and social events.

It was both very dystopian and very Damascus. It was both terrible and beautiful.

The beauty came in the way we got up every morning, pushed back the curtains, and stood in awe of the waking sky. The gifts looked like time for rest, reflection, and connection—even if from a six-foot distance. We recommitted ourselves to game nights and home-cooked meals. We lit taper candles and thought it would be fun to use the fine china. We shot hoops with the kids, put together puzzles, caught up on favorite podcasts.

Maybe you took long, slow walks with your dogs and learned how to knit. Perhaps you taught Grandma how to do a Zoom call and dropped off groceries on the doorstep of your elderly neighbor. You hopefully reordered your life and found out that good things can grow out of the soil of adversity.

Even if we were busier than ever before (nodding to the doctors and nurses here), we likely paid attention to the world around us in ways we hadn't in a really long time, maybe never. We saw Earth working the way God made her to. The sun rose and set on time, like it always had, like a banner of hope and resilience. Nature healed us. Seasons soothed us. We believed, once more, that we were part of something far, far bigger than ourselves.

In our state of enforced slowness, we were living a Growing Slow mindset.

For those of us who were considered "non-essential," and therefore mandated to "shelter in place," Growing Slow became a way of life. Things we once thought impossible were suddenly possible—things like carving out time to really be present with ourselves. The calendar opened up. You had the weird luxury of time to teach your daughter how to embroider a dishtowel and to read an extra chapter of your Bible every morning. You looked at the month ahead and saw only a smattering of appointments.

Perhaps the greatest—and most uncomfortable—gift came when we had a plain, unobstructed view of ourselves. Because in time, the novelty and adrenaline wore off. The strange quiet of inactivity began to echo around us, and we grew tired of the same meals, the same four walls. For the first time in forever, we remembered what it was to be bored. This new way of life exposed our coping mechanisms, along with the things we secretly worshipped. Those were the things that have kept us from adopting a Growing Slow mindset for our entire lives: productivity, busyness, comfort, security, achievement, the metrics-based growth that has hurried our hearts for years.

These forced moments of reevaluation held value.

Early on, I knew I didn't want to go back to my old way of living, where I too often tied self-worth to productivity, where I was too quick to consume and discard. This accidental farm girl had long been learning lessons from the farm on un-hurrying the heart. Those lessons were magnified during the pandemic, and I didn't want to forget. The land—with its resilience in the setting sun, the moving clouds, the first geese returning north—was healing us at the roots.

There was one thing that made me nervous about life getting back to "normal," whatever normal was. I was nervous that I would return to old habits. In the urgency to get back to normal living, I had to ask myself, what parts of "normal" did I want to leave behind? I didn't want "old normal." Many of us began asking ourselves, "When this is all over, how will we be better people?"

For me, the answer came down to a list of five things I can't afford to forget.

1. It's healthy to be in the "right here, right now."

I've prided myself on being a long-range planner. But the inability to plan too far ahead was a strange and needed gift. We never knew when restrictions would be lifted. We didn't know whether we could hold graduations, weddings, or even church. This was both immensely frustrating and deeply transformative. For years, I have wanted to live "in the now," but it always seemed like a lofty, impractical ideal. And then, the whole world screeched to a halt. We were compelled to live in terms of minutes and hours instead of days and weeks. More than any time in recent history, we learned what it meant to live "in the now." This is a cornerstone belief of the Growing Slow mindset, and I believe it's possible to carry this ideal into our post-pandemic lives.

Our un-hurried hearts have suffered too long under freeway speeds as we rush toward long-term benchmarks. We're scared to take the back roads, thinking we won't get where we need to be. Friend, you are right where you need to be, right here and right now. And the *right now* holds so much loveliness, not the least of which is a deeper understanding that God actually is running the show down here on planet Earth.

Make your plans, absolutely. But rather than wrapping your fists tightly around those plans, hold them loosely, and lift them all up to God in open, cupped hands.

We can make our plans, but the LORD determines our steps.[1]

2. Nature never hurries.

Before the pandemic, my trips out to the yard had a stiff practicality: feed the cats, pull the weeds, scoop the snow, trim the bushes, walk to the edge of the field to deliver lunch to my favorite farmer.

After we were forced into quarantine, trips outside became an act of pure delight, even reverence. I made it a practice to open the door, step outside, put my bare feet on solid ground, and tip my face to the heavens. Every single day. Under a big sky, I would close my eyes and feel the warmth of the sun, the pelting of rain, or the sting of sleet. No matter the weather, I felt a strong pull to step outside and behold a shred of God's magnificence. Sunsets and shimmering starlight reminded me of God's steadfastness. My lungs inflating with fresh air made me feel more alive, more human than ever before. We were all tuned into the natural rhythms that God set into motion from the beginning, rather than the false rhythms we created to advance our purposes.

We stepped into it, and we all paid attention to the call of the wild, whether we lived on a farm in Iowa or two blocks from the city park.

Elizabeth Barrett Browning once wrote:

> Earth's crammed with heaven,
> And every common bush afire with God,
> But only he who sees takes off his shoes;
> The rest sit round and pluck blackberries.

We don't want to go back to merely plucking berries and pruning roses. Nature serves more than a utilitarian function. Land is more than a thing to be plowed, planted, fertilized, plucked, and harvested. Like people, the natural world's value is far greater than its outputs. This grand old earth is a treasure to be enjoyed, and she serves as a megaphone of God's great love for us.

If God went to all this trouble to make Earth so beautiful, we should step into her beauty and say thank you. Our family is the only family who has this very view of this very slice of the world— where the pheasants run through the evergreens and the field rolls north as far as the eye can see, where an eagle dives to grab its lunch and the blackest dirt yields food for a hungry world. If we don't thank God for it, who will? Let's stand outside, turn our eyes to our own patch of sky, and soak in every trace of God's beauty.

From the beginning, nature has embodied a Growing Slow mindset. It never hurries. It always heals.

3. A scarcity mindset breeds panic. A Growing Slow mindset promotes peace.

Think back to the times when you couldn't find what you needed at the store—whether that was hand sanitizer or disinfecting wipes. Several theories evolved over why we couldn't find what we needed. Certainly, "panic buying" was at play. When people believe that resources are dwindling, there's a sudden rush to get more, even if you actually have enough to get by for a while. This is what's called a *scarcity mindset*.

We observed two kinds of attitudes during the pandemic— attitudes that propagated a scarcity mindset, and attitudes that propagated a Growing Slow mindset.

A scarcity mindset rushes to get more, to acquire excess. A Growing Slow mindset takes only what is needed.

A scarcity mindset believes there will never be enough. A Growing Slow mindset trusts there will be more.

A scarcity mindset is about hurrying and hustling. A Growing Slow mindset is about un-hurrying your heart and finding the peace you've always longed for.

These mindsets apply not only during worldwide pandemics, but any time we are tempted to operate out of a fear of lack. Our mindset influences how we use our time and resources. It influences our relationships with both our competitors and our colleagues.

It greatly impacts how we carry out a key teaching of Jesus: "Love your neighbor as yourself."[2]

In those early days of the pandemic, I observed good people coming alongside others facing shortages. One night, I received a text from a pastor in a nearby city. His congregation was made up mostly of Sudanese refugee families, and they had run out of toilet paper. He asked if our church could help. Frankly, many of us were in the same boat. But in a fishes and loaves moment, we were able to gather enough toilet paper to share with people in need. Later, when members of that same congregation tested positive for the virus, we came together to buy their groceries. That's the power of a Growing Slow mindset that assumes abundance instead of scarcity.

As we un-hurry our hearts, let's not forget the responsibility we have to each other. If we are constantly on the run, we will miss Jesus' command to take care of our neighbors.

4. The Ancient Way of Growing Slow is a rescue boat on the sea of uncertainty.

"For everything there is a season, and a time for every matter under heaven."[3] This has always been the Ancient Way of Growing Slow: trusting that God keeps the seasons in motion.

During the pandemic, different seasons happened simultaneously. On the same day, one friend birthed a child, and another friend grieved her father's death. "A time to be born, and a time to die."[4]

Dear friends were planning private funerals, while my own children were making delightful TikTok dances to show their grandparents. "A time to mourn, and a time to dance."[5]

Hard seasons usually last longer than we like, and in those moments of adversity, the Ancient Way of Growing Slow becomes a lifeboat on rough seas. "The only way out is through," as they say. And calmer days will come.

During the pandemic, my best friend, Michelle, showed up at my door to drop off groceries. She's an incredibly thoughtful soul, and in typical fashion, she left a bouquet of flowers along with the grocery sacks. She was halfway down my sidewalk by the time I made it to the door, and when I opened it, she turned around to face me. There were tears rolling down her cheeks. The weight of everything happening in our world was hitting her hard.

We stared at each other, and tears welled up in my eyes, too. My "hugger" instincts fired up in a hurry, and I made a move toward Michelle, without even thinking. She held out a hand, in a stop motion, as if to say, "No, you can't."

It was heartbreaking. We just stared at each other, six feet apart and wordless, as the tears fell.

I never imagined a world where I couldn't hug my best friend. But that's the world we lived in for a time. It's part of the Ancient Way. There is, indeed, "a time to embrace and a time to refrain from embracing."[6]

A few months earlier, I had a hard time imagining when I would ever refrain from embracing. And suddenly, there we were, kept apart by the threat of a virus.

In that moment, I promised myself never to take seasons of embracing for granted. We ought to wrap our arms around those we love and hold them so tight. So very tight.

5. Everything that we always had in Christ is still ours.

When troubles come in this life, and they will, we cannot forget the hope we have in Christ.

Our security is not in our hustle.

Our security is not in our productivity.

Our security is not in our earthly comfort.

Our security is not in our health.

Our security is not in a perfect schedule.

Our security is not in the latest decluttering system we bought on the internet.

Our security is in the unchangeable assurance of Christ alone.

Every trial we face will be made right in Christ. Every unproductive season produces fruit inside of us.

We actually have everything we need, and we don't lose it when hell breaks loose on earth. And that's not something I *think*. It's something I *believe* because God said so: "His divine power has given us *everything we need*."[7]

Some of the hardest seasons we endure last a very long time. When we are in the middle of them, we find ourselves saying, "Things will never be the same after this." And maybe that's a good thing. Because did we really want more of the same? Did we want to go back to business as usual?

If we are honest, most of us haven't valued people and connection as much as we should. Most of us have been afraid of getting behind, so we refused to rest. Most of us were putting off the most important things until tomorrow. But we aren't guaranteed tomorrow. Everything we treasure most can be gone in a moment.

Think, for a moment, back to the beginning moments of COVID-19. We experienced incredible things we never saw or heard before—a pride of lions napping on a South African road, birds chirping louder than ever before in Manhattan. Or maybe they always were singing like that, and we just didn't slow down enough to hear them.

It's time to make a change. We can let the upending of everything reorder the whole of our lives. Or we can go back to where we were.

Which will we choose?

REMEMBER

Un-hurrying our hearts requires the
breaking down of old habits and the
building up of new and sustainable ones.

REFLECT

How did COVID-19 change your life?

With everything that changed that year, what were the
unchangeable things you held onto?

Amid uncertainty, what got you through?

What destructive practices did you let go of?

RETURN

At the end of each chapter,
we return to the soil.

Times of suffering tend to reveal two things: what we treasure and what we fear. What do you treasure? What do you fear? What did you learn that season that you don't want to forget? Our answers to these questions will inform what we choose to plant in our fields every single day. Take a moment to pray for your priority seeds today.

CHAPTER 19

A TIME TO DANCE

The most memorable surprise party I ever attended had an interesting twist. Trish, the honored guest, helped plan it, not realizing until the night of the party that all of this planning was to celebrate her.

Months before, Trish had been diagnosed with pancreatic cancer and had been fighting cancer like a boss. We wanted to find a way to celebrate her trademark zest for life, but knowing she didn't like being the center of attention, we had to get creative. So we cooked up an elaborate party that she helped plan.

Trish is a huge fan of *Downton Abbey*, a TV series that chronicles the lives of an aristocratic family and their servants in early twentieth-century England. So we schemed to bring a little Downton Abbey to a shed tucked between two Iowa farm fields. My best friend, Michelle, and her husband, Rob, spent weeks transforming their farm shed into an abbey. They built a fireplace surround out of cardboard, built backdrops, and planned a menu even Violet Crawley would approve of.

We gathered up every vintage dress and bow tie and china cup and candelabra we could find. Night after night, Trish showed up at the shed with another fake ficus tree or a set of brass candlesticks.

We had told her the party was being held in honor of some friends from Great Britain who were coming to Iowa for a visit. That was not true, of course. Not only are we great surprise party throwers, we are splendid liars.

The night of the party came. Everyone showed up at the shed dressed as characters from the show. Trish came as Mrs. Patmore; I was her sidekick, Daisy.

And then came the great reveal. We were lined up inside the shed, creating a long aisle for the Great Britain "guests" to walk through when they arrived. A great hush fell on the crowd when the butler, played by my husband, stepped out of line with a silver tray resting delicately upon his properly gloved hands. Atop the tray was a "telegram" for Rob, the lord of the house.

With a great flourish and a hilarious British accent, the telegram was read, announcing that the guests from the UK would not be coming after all but that they sent their regards to Mrs. Patmore.

It took a moment for Trish, a.k.a. Mrs. Patmore, to realize what was happening, but when she did, we commenced with singing and dancing and eating and laughing and all kinds of ridiculosity. It was, in a word, magical.

That moment for me stands as a vivid reminder of the importance of celebration, laughter, and the value of play, even as adults. Partying is a lost art. We rarely take a beat to celebrate accomplishments, big or small. And the joy of life itself? Well, when do we ever celebrate *that*? We reach a goal and immediately start calculating how to accomplish the next one. We cross off everything on our to-do lists and immediately start writing new ones.

Our souls were made for celebration, for expressions of deep happiness, air guitars, and dance-offs.

Hurry wounds the happy heart of celebration. Hurry pushes us headlong toward the planting of spring, the growing of summer, and the harvest of autumn. But for one-fourth of an entire year, nature calls us into winter. When winter hits, we look around, and we imagine that nothing good is happening because it's dreary, cold, and unproductive.

Perhaps the winter seasons of our lives have a hidden purpose. Perhaps they were made to be lit up with the candlelight of celebration. God created winter—a built-in period of time to pause and reflect, perhaps even to be a little ridiculous with our friends while harmonizing to '80s music.

Renowned Christian author Richard J. Foster suggests that celebration is an important spiritual discipline, alongside prayer, fasting, meditation, and study.

> Far and away the most important benefit of celebration is that it saves us from taking ourselves too seriously. That is a desperately needed grace for all those who are earnest about the Spiritual Disciplines. It is an occupational hazard of devout folk to become stuffy bores. That should not be. Of all people, we should be the most free, alive, interesting. Celebration adds a note of gaiety, festivity, hilarity to our lives. After all, Jesus rejoiced so fully in life that He was accused of being a winebibber and a glutton. Many of us lead such sour lives that we couldn't possibly be accused of such things.[1]

Without a joyful spirit of celebration and festivity, Foster says, our "disciplines become dull, death-breathing tools in the hands of modern Pharisees."[2]

Without winter seasons of the soul, our lives easily slip into patterns set by metrics. Without winter, we might never take time to see the value of what we've already harvested. We must change the way we see winter—not as a season to be rushed through, but as a season to be savored. Winter has long undergone a case of mistaken identity. It is not merely a time to mourn, but a place to turn our mourning into dancing.

The Bible beckons us to celebrate as a body. Moments of celebration are sprinkled throughout Scriptures. Recall the shepherds, wise men, and angels celebrating the birth of Christ. In the Old Testament, time was set aside for celebration festivals and feasts. Toward the end of the biblical narrative, we are invited to an epic celebration: the wedding of the Lamb.

Celebration and joy are at the heart of a Growing Slow mindset. Indeed, they are at the center of the un-hurried heart of Christ.

Jesus, said, "These things I have spoken to you that my joy may be in you, and that your joy may be full."[3]

Come, Let Us Koselig

It's possible to recover a sense of joviality in the winter of life.

Have you heard of the small Norwegian island called Tromsø? It sits north of the Arctic Circle, where the polar night lasts from November to January. In such darkness and cold, it's hard to imagine what it would be like to carry a heart of celebration. But the residents who live there defy expectations. Social psychologist Kari Leibowitz, who studied the people of Tromsø in 2015, discovered that, instead of dreading those slow and dark days, they embraced the days as *koselig*, the Norwegian word for "cozy."

"Candles were everywhere, in homes, cafes, and even offices. The town glowed. Residents got outside to hike or go to cabins or ski to work. They gathered for potlucks. They threw festivals. Life moved more slowly, but it was no less fulfilling and actually more fun than the summer months."[4]

What would it be like if we took intentional steps every day to bring a little light and *koselig* to our winter moments? What would it be like to gather around the table and light the candles? Let's make our towns and villages glow. Let's step outside, under bare branches on the crispest of mornings, and breathe in cool air. Let's light little fires in our stone pits and in our hearts, snuggle under fuzzy blankets, and drink from warm cups. Let's connect more deeply with God and our people. Let's come alive to moments of thanksgiving.

We typically think of celebrations during the seasons when our hearts don't necessarily need it most: graduations in spring, weddings, block parties, and picnics in summer.

But perhaps we need celebrations most in the winter.

An un-hurried heart leads to moments of intentional celebration—even in unexpected winter. An un-hurried heart embodies the Ancient Way of Growing Slow, believing that God is in the business of making all things beautiful in their time.

As we move across the land, across seasons—from a farm in Eden to a forever farm in heaven—let's find the good things growing here, even in winter. Let's hold on to the vision of a future where God makes everything beautiful as we move toward the grandest celebration of all.

One Long Table under a Great Big Sky

I have a recurring dream. In it, there's a long table stretching out under an open sky. The heavens are coated with stars, so many stars that we don't need to light the ivory tapers someone twisted into crystal holders. The table is covered in a white cloth that blows in the breeze, and all the people are laughing and carrying on.

I carry pottery heaped high with steaming food to that long rectangle in the grass. My hands smell like garlic, and the air smells like lilacs.

I'm not wearing shoes, because I want to feel the grass between my toes when I walk back and forth to the kitchen.

The little boys are burping. Some of the women are dressed in sequined gowns, like they got all gussied for some ball to be held in some marbled room somewhere. Sitting beside them are new friends who came wearing dirty, threadbare T-shirts with screen-printed sayings like, "Go Wildcats" or "Life is Good." Someone parked a Mercedes next to a rusty Pinto. I nearly trip over a pair of crutches propped up near the head of the table.

There's this rich tapestry of faces—ebony, creamy white, olive, cocoa—and everyone is smiling and carrying on like old friends because all the bad things got made right somehow.

Everyone got invited, and almost everyone came. We hoped and prayed that they would. We wanted them to taste the feast. And we know for sure that someone hoped and prayed for us, too.

There was an awareness hanging in the air: it cost someone a lot to make a space for us at the table.

We came with empty pockets, because the Host told us that this was all a gift.

The price of admission? Our hunger.

In the dream, a bunch of us had taped a sign to a barrel and rolled it out to the middle of Main Street, just like they always do in our town when there's something to celebrate: Come One and All! The poor, the lame, the drunk, the rich, the holy. The naughty kid, the valedictorian, the blind guy, the beggar, and the CEO.

There was room for all of us, and all of us had been waiting our whole lives for this. We just didn't know it until now.

The table seems intimate—like it could fit in the corner of some small diner—yet it stretches for miles because the Host didn't pick favorites. He wants us all.

When I touch the table, it feels like it has a heartbeat.

From the grass, I watch them come 'round the corner, out by the wizened oaks. Some have tears in their eyes. A guy in a three-piece suit drops to his knees on the sidewalk when he sees a chair with his name on the back of it. An old woman throws back her head and starts singing a song I've never heard before, but somehow, I know all the words. There's a poem hanging from the branches of a tree, and music slides down from the sky. It falls like dew on our skin. Fireflies dance around our heads.

We wear no masks. We showed up fragile and hungry. We are safe here. We are happy—the fullest happiness we have ever known. Or maybe we had simply forgotten that this kind of happiness was possible because of all the pain in the busted-up, fast-moving world we'd been living in.

"Bring your mess," says the banner flapping in the breeze. "Your mess doesn't disqualify you. It's your ticket in."

We all know we are a mess, and when we get to thinking about it, we are astonished at the invitation to a table so sacred. The Host lets us help serve the dinner, which floors me. And so we keep bringing out potatoes and green beans and filet mignon, and my hands shake a little at the honor of carrying food to the table.

There is more than enough for everyone.

In the dream, the Host clears his throat, and the sound echoes down the table, a hallowed rumble. He says, "Have a seat please." We all find a place at the table. A holy silence falls around our ears, and then down to our ankles.

Everyone is barefoot, and all the bare feet are under one long table, and that's the part that makes me cry every time.

REMEMBER

Hurry wounds the happy
heart of celebration.

REFLECT

Does it feel possible to celebrate anything when you are
in a winter season of the heart?

....

....

How does a hurried heart keep us from practicing
celebration and gratitude?

....

....

....

....

What's one thing you can do today to keep from falling
into the "occupational hazard of devout folk (becoming)
stuffy bores"?

....

....

....

....

RETURN

At the end of each chapter,
we return to the soil.

Put your bare feet on the ground beneath that giant table. Whose feet are next to yours? The most important seeds we plant while we are on earth are the seeds we plant in other people, helping them grow into the knowledge of an eternity with Christ. Let's invite more people to the table. Make a list of people you'd like to include.

CHAPTER 20

HEAVEN LOOKS LIKE A FARM

Today was the perfect kind of day. This morning, I brought Scott his sack lunch and sat in the tractor, on the "buddy seat," as he disked the field west of the house. Disking is a springtime ritual to prepare the land for planting, and it always feels like holy work— turning the soil over, burying old earth underneath the new.

After my tractor ride, I took the girls for a surprise picnic in the park. We sat cross-legged on a blanket and ate sandwiches and oranges. The sun warmed our backs through our T-shirts. After we ate, we sought shade under a giant oak. The tree hadn't yet leafed out, but the branches were so thick, so broad, that they cast giant, veiny shadows on the earth.

As Earth tilts herself back toward spring, I keep thinking of old words I wrote on my blog not long after we'd moved here, when the girls were barely out of diapers:

> I've only recently begun to realize how we've been grafted into this cycle of family and its link to Earth. Before we came home, we never lived anywhere long enough to see our lives come full circle with seasons. We moved from place to place, career to career, groping for more of something we couldn't quite name.

But we abandoned that grasping at air in order to settle in a cycle of greater substance. We are daily brought humbly low to the dirt, the very substance God used to form man. We are from dirt, working the dirt, waking up dirt. And in these fields—farmed by the hands of Lee men who've come before—we plant in the dirt.

We prepare the soil for the seed and trust God to do something new in this season that eternally blooms with hope and new beginnings.

We've come home.

Those journaled longings for a Growing Slow life echo forward to find me right here, as we stand on the edge of spring, you and me. All seasons and all life, under God, come full circle.

"We've come home," I wrote.

How do those words settle in your soul right now?

Earth and her seasons have so much to teach us, and I am still learning what it means to be true kin to those who cared for this land centuries before us, and to those who will care for it long after we're gone. God has woven the land into our family's story, and he has woven the land into your story, too. You belong to God's good earth, and one day, we will live together in a new and glorious earth.

It's already promised, and here we are—living in the already *and* the not yet. We wait with hope while living in a place of drought and tears and winter storms that interrupt the fresh start of spring.

Remember when I told you that people around here joke that if you don't like the weather, wait a day? It's true. Driving home from our picnic, I listened to the weatherman on the radio, who said there would be several inches of snow on the ground by Easter morning.

To everything there is a season, and sometimes those seasons will give you whiplash—the hope of spring followed by winter's attempt at a last stand. Moments of unbridled joy interrupted by a deep and unexpected sadness. Seasons of new birth disrupted by an untimely death. A Good Friday followed by a Resurrection Sunday. Crosses next to empty tombs because you can't have the one without the other.

As I write, it's Holy Week. And this is a Holy Week unlike any you and I have experienced in our lifetimes. This was the year when none of us could worship in our own churches during these high and holy days, because of a pandemic. Do you recall the strange comfort of knowing that—as devastating as it was—we were all in this together, carrying our joy and our suffering to the cross? On Easter Sunday, millions of us gathered around screens in our homes, worshipping a Risen Savior who assures us that he has victory over viruses and disappointments and unexpected seasons and cancer and anxiety and tombs. Once upon a time, we used to argue about silly things, like whether Communion should be taken with wine or grape juice. Suddenly, a pandemic upended everything, and the "Body of Christ, given for you" became a hamburger bun or a stale saltine cracker. The "Blood of Christ, shed for you" was a tiny cup of apple juice, thrown to the back of your throat, while you wore slippers and pajamas. Our pastor kept telling us that Jesus—when he instituted Communion—would have used common elements from the table where he reclined. And somehow that made everything feel okay—to use ordinary elements found in the back of the pantry to fill our spiritual hunger.

A virus can keep people out of church buildings, but it can't keep Christ out of the world or out of us. He sat with us, in that suspended state of enforced slowness when we communed with crackers and juice boxes. He held us, with our traumatized hearts and our ache to embrace our grandmothers. Easter never stops coming. The grave stays empty. God does not abandon us, no matter what season we find ourselves in. This is, and always shall be, the Ancient Way of Growing Slow.

The assurance of an unchangeable Savior is everything. Seasons change. Bodies change. The faces of the people in front of us change. Circumstances change. Relationships change. Fields change. Seeds change.

But Jesus never changes. And everything we always had in him is still ours today.

Today, our unchangeable Jesus met me in the tractor and in the park and under the oak, and now at my desk, overlooking a field that has become your friend now, as well as mine. Right now, I am thinking of you because I have a single task this afternoon: to find a handful of words to offer as we come to the end of this dusty road.

My job today is to cast a vision for what life can be when we stop running and stand still. To tell you, one last time, that meaningful change is possible in every part of our lives—our relationships, businesses, faith—when we willingly Grow Slow.

Because it is.

It's possible.

This is what I want to tell you: I have expended far too much time, energy, and financial resources trying to figure out how to move faster toward a spectacular life. I nearly lost a sense of the mattering things as my life screamed along like a freight train. I was years, maybe months, from losing myself to the rush of "too much to do and too little time to do it."

And then, in the most un-spectacular place—a regular old farm—I found a settledness I didn't even know was possible. It came in a whisper on a dirt road, in the turning of earth, during the harvests that came despite all odds. It came in moments under our country steeple, in meeting people like Wayne and Kim, with their notepad of future dinner guests. It came in the way the sun kept rising, and kept setting, and then rising again—the Ancient Way.

Hand to the sky, I am being delivered from an un-hurried heart.

I am finding joy in simple pleasures and purpose in simple work. I still work hard, but I can do so without leaking toxic waste all over the people I love. I can be lazy on a Monday without feeling guilty.

I have found a way to live without panic and am enjoying a new and steady peace right where I am—not on the freeway of life, but at the end of a dusty country lane, where my hands get dirty.

I slowed down, and behold, I discovered that I hadn't disappointed God after all.

One goal I've had since Jesus rescued my soul is to hear, "Well done." By Growing Slow, I learned that he doesn't want to tell me "Well done" based on the quality of my harvest. He wants to tell me "Well done" for my obedience in the planting.

Hear Jesus speaking to you, right where you are. Don't miss this:

> "Listen carefully. Unless a grain of wheat is buried in the ground, dead to the world, it is never any more than a grain of wheat. But if it is buried, it sprouts and reproduces itself many times over. In the same way, anyone who holds on to life just as it is destroys that life. But if you let it go, reckless in your love, you'll have it forever, real and eternal."[1]

Friend, this is your moment. This is your here and now. The seeds in your hands are meant to be planted. Let them go. Be reckless in your love.

Jesus says that unless you put the seed in the ground, nothing will happen. But if you do? It will multiply.

For a while, it will look like nothing is happening. But one day, with great strength, green growth will shoot forth. A seed that was actually dead will make life. But it's not this fact alone that is so impressive. It's *how much* life springs forth.

On our farm, a single seed of corn in spring produces 600 kernels by autumn. Think about it. One single seed grows up and creates 600 kernels. Added up, a whole field produces millions upon millions of kernels.

The seeds you are planting produce more than you could ever know.

Do you see it for yourself, friend?

Do you see it right where you are, at the edge of the field where God placed you? Spring is comin' 'round again, and you've got fistfuls of seeds in those work-worn hands of yours. Slip off your shoes and feel the earth, solid under your feet. Let this moment ground you.

Look beside you. My bare feet are right beside yours now. You've spent an entire book visiting my fields; today, I've come to yours. Up above, there's this gorgeous blue sky. The soil has been turned over, and the seed bed is ready.

And today, I have come here, to your fields, for a commissioning.

A Commission to Grow Slow

I commission you, not in my strength, but in the power of Earth's first Farmer, our Lord, who has called us to bear fruit—fruit that lasts.

I commission you to enter your fields.

I commission you to plant, tend, nurture, grow, and bring in the sheaves, just as you have been doing. I commission you to go out and do the incredible work you've been doing all along, at the pace of a regular person and not an Olympic sprinter.

You have so much permission right here. You have permission to stop building something bigger and faster. You have permission to stop multitasking yourself to the brink of exhaustion. You have permission to live a quiet, less benchmark-y life. You have permission, even, to be unproductive.

I pray that you will know, deep down within yourself, how precious you are. You are beyond price, beyond compare. Your worth is not tied to your speed or success rate. Do you see what a wonder you are? Oh, I pray you do.

May you never again ask yourself a question like, "Does this even matter at all?"

It all matters.

The little things are the mattering things. The times you dropped everything to show up for the weary friend. The times you paced the hallways, in the dark, with a fussy baby in your arms. The times you read one more bedtime story, sent one more heartfelt text message, gave one more dollar, read one more verse, offered one more minute of your time, pulled out one more chair, planted one more seed. Oh, friend, it mattered. It matters still. These are the "well done" things.

Awaken to the reckless love you were made for.

Let your soul open up, so wide, so stretched out—wide as a country sky—that it makes you cry.

May you have the courage to grow slow. May you know that when you grow slow, you grow deep.

Stop waiting for someone to validate the things you are growing in those fields of yours. Someone already has.

Stop defining your goals by the success in someone else's field. God knows exactly where you are supposed to be.

And may you never, ever forget for a single second that God enjoys watching you grow slow. He isn't upset or disappointed that sanctification takes time.

There's no doubt about it, sister. You are a farmer. But you are also a field—a glorious, blooming, wild, unruly, and wonderful field.

You are worth every bit of seed planted into you.

And these seeds, they are already growing good things.

The land is woven into your story.

Once upon a time, on a farm called Eden where good things

grew, God knelt down, cupped dirt in his hand, breathed life into humankind, and made us all.

We are on our way to a new land, the promised land, across the Jordan.

The last pages of the Good Book tell us there's going to be a great big shining city, a new Jerusalem, waiting for us when we wake up in heaven someday. Maybe we'll wake up to a gate made of pearls or a street paved in gold.

Maybe.

But I believe plenty of us are going to wake up on a big ol' blissful farm called Eden.[2] There will be rolling hills and towering trees, puffy clouds, and a bunch of rocking chairs pointed west. There will be laughter and dancing and picnics in the greenest yard you've ever seen. Patchwork quilts will be spread out on the ground, and atop them, brimming baskets of cheese, warm bread, and finest wine. Ladybugs will crawl up blades of grass, and lambs will be resting next to lions. A crystal river will run straight down the middle.

Never again will we worry about drought or sorrow or cancer or divorce or death or some impending darkness looming on the horizon. God himself will light up every corner, forevermore, on a farm with no more night.

Can you see it?

This is the promised land, and it's the place where we belong. A place to call home.

Until then, here you are—at the edge of a field that hints at your forever.

This is your land.

It's not perfect, but it is good. Really good.

It's your turn. Kneel down now. Carve a line in the dirt with your finger. Pluck a seed from your fist, and lay it gently in your soil.

This is where it all begins.

Grow slow, my friend. Grow slow.

ACKNOWLEDGMENTS

If you were to drive the country roads where I live, you'd think farming was a solitary, lonesome way of life. Houses sit far apart from one another. Churches and stores are miles away from our front doors.

But the truth is, despite the distance, a farmer doesn't farm alone. Farming is all about community, teamwork, and belonging. A farmer's team includes agronomists, bankers, and seed dealers. Farmers keep an eye on each other's property. If your cattle get loose, a neighbor will help you round them up. Around here, if a farmer gets sick, another farmer will step in to harvest the crops.

We take care of the land, and we take care of each other. It's the Farmer Way.

That's the way it is with book writing too. Each word is a seed planted, watered, prayed for, and tended by a community. To each of you who walked with me through this *Growing Slow* field, I offer my deepest thanks.

I thank God for you, and for these:

To Scott, my favorite farmer. The lessons we've learned together, toward un-hurried living, were hard earned. Thank you for allowing me to share a story that is not just mine, but ours. I'll never forget how, after chores many nights, you'd settle into your recliner with my manuscript. You read new chapters, advised me on technical farming references, and opened my eyes to biblical passages that enriched the message. You are my first editor, my closest confidant, my best friend, my safe place, and the love of my life.

To our parents. Growing up, we probably took for granted the slow pace, the sameness, the wide-open spaces, and the hidden beauty of the ordinary. Thank you for not saying, "I told you so" when we eventually came back home.

To Lydia and Anna. You were my motivation to adopt a Growing Slow mindset. I never wanted to look back at your growing-up years and see only a blur of memory. I know I'm not a perfect mom, but I hope that through all the tuck-ins, silly tea parties, spontaneous road trips, inside jokes, and heartfelt prayers, you've felt my love, love, love.

To Rob and Michelle. Your friendship is one of our favorite parts of living here. We hold dear the hundreds of times that we've "listened to the sun set" while sitting next to you. Let's keep on livin' off love and the land.

To Lisa Jackson. You are an agent, a counselor, a wordsmith, and a friend. You saw the merit of this book before I did.

To Stephanie Smith. You are incomparable. Crops need light and water to grow, and in a way, so do books. God used you to bring both light and water to every page of *Growing Slow*—light to illuminate the message, and water to parch the soul of every weary and thirsty reader.

To Harmony, Stefanie, Alicia, and the rest of the Zondervan team. Thank you for helping me carry this message from the farm to the world. There would be no harvest from this little crop of words if it weren't for you.

To Kaitlyn Bouchillon. I am grateful for your friendship, creativity, and your work behind the scenes to make my online ministry vibrant and sustainable. And like I've told you a dozen times, I don't ever want to launch a book without you by my side.

To Christine Waldner and Infini Films. Thank you for helping me tell the story of *Growing Slow* through video so we can visually convey this important message through screens around the world.

To Anjuli Paschall. Your insights provided breakthrough when I didn't know what I was trying to say. Your wisdom was invaluable!

To my (in)courage sisters and Hope*Writers. You are a constant source of friendship, encouragement, and inspiration.

To the generous-hearted, longtime readers of my books, my social media posts, and JenniferDukesLee.com. Thank you for your emails, for your encouragement, and for your friendship. I want you to know I don't see this relationship as transactional. This is a sisterhood, and you are why I write.

And to you, God, the first Farmer. You knelt down in the dirt, on a farm called Eden, and breathed life into us all. It slays me how you seem to enjoy watching us grow—little by little—until we reach the fullness of all you created us to be. You could have brought us to full maturity with the snap of your fingers, but instead you call us to a life that moves us forward an inch at a time. Thank you for love, for life, and for the audacious permission to grow slow.

NOTES

A Note to the Reader

1. Christina Rossetti, "In the Bleak Midwinter," in *The New English Hymnal* (Norwich, UK: Canterbury Press, 1986), 60.

Introduction

1. Matt. 6:28
2. Geir Berthelsen, "Geir Berthelsen's Ten-Point Guide to Going Slow," The World Institute of Slowness, https://www.theworldinstituteofslowness.com/geir-berthelsens-ten-point-guide-to-going-slow/.
3. Ann Fisher, "Too Busy to Think? You May Suffer from 'Hurry Sickness,'" Fortune.com, February 4, 2015, https://fortune.com/2015/02/04/busy-hurry-work-stress/.
4. Paul H. Wright, *Understanding the Ecology of the Bible: An Introductory Atlas* (Jerusalem: Carta Jerusalem, 2018), 6.
5. Eccl. 3:1 NKJV

Chapter 1: Permission to Be Un-Spectacular

1. Bill Heatley, "Background on Colossae and the Colossians," Theology of Work Project, January 11, 2010, https://www.theologyofwork.org/new-testament/colossians-philemon/introduction-to-colossians-and-philemon/background-on-colossae-and-the-colossians.

2. Col. 2:6–7 NLT
3. In his internationally bestselling book *In Praise of Slowness* (HarperOne 2005), Carl Honore coined the phrase, "The Slow Movement."
4. Matt. 11:28–30 MSG

Chapter 2: We Are All Farmers

1. Gen. 2:8
2. Gen. 2:15
3. Gen. 2:19
4. Gen. 3:5
5. Gen. 3:23
6. Deut. 8:7–8
7. Ex. 33:14
8. 1 Peter 1:3
9. Mark 4:26–27, emphasis mine.

Chapter 3: We Are Also Fields

1. 1 Cor. 3:9
2. Ps. 147:10 NLT
3. Matt. 23:14 NKJV
4. Phil. 3:14
5. 2 Peter 3:18 MSG
6. Matt. 13:21 MSG
7. Matt. 13:8 MSG
8. Hab. 2:3 TLB

Chapter 4: The Ancient Way of Growing Slow

1. Eccl. 3:1–8 ESV
2. Eccl. 3:11
3. John 12:24 GW
4. Anjuli Paschall, *Stay: Discovering Grace, Freedom, and Wholeness Where You Never Imagined Looking* (Bloomington, MN: Bethany House, 2020), 190.

Chapter 6: You Are Not Falling Behind

1. Rom. 8:26
2. 1 Cor. 15:58 ESV
3. Gal. 6:9 MSG
4. Acts 1:6
5. Acts 1:7–8 MSG
6. Mark 4:26–27, emphasis added.

Chapter 7: Built to Last

1. Gaia Vince, "The High Cost of Our Throwaway Culture," BBC, November 28, 2012, https://www.bbc.com/future/article /20121129-the-cost-of-our-throwaway-culture.
2. 1 Cor. 3:9 GNT, emphasis added.
3. 2 Peter 3:9
4. Ps. 102:18

Chapter 8: The Little Things Are the Big Things

1. 1 Cor. 2:9 ESV

Chapter 9: What It All Comes Down To

1. Eph. 2:8
2. Luke 5:16
3. Deut. 31:6 ESV
4. Matt. 28:20 ESV
5. Rom. 8:38–39 ESV
6. The concept of reparenting is explored in David Eckman's *Knowing the Heart of the Father* (Eugene, OR: Harvest House, 2008).

Chapter 10: Good Fences

1. Prov. 25:28
2. Emily P. Freeman, *The Next Right Thing* (Grand Rapids, MI: Revell, 2019), 178.
3. This phrasing is used repeatedly in the Bible, including (but

not limited to) 1 Kings 15:26, 1 Kings 15:34, 1 Kings 16:25, and 1 Kings 22:52.
4. This phrasing is used repeatedly in the Bible, including (but not limited to) 1 Kings 15:11, 2 Kings 12:2, and 2 Kings 15:3.
5. 2 Chron. 26:4 ESV
6. 2 Chron. 26:10
7. 2 Chron. 26:15

Chapter 11: The One Where We Grow Slow with Friends

1. This quote is most often attributed to Maya Angelou.
2. Col. 2:7 MSG

Chapter 12: When a Dream Dies

1. Deut. 4:21–22
2. Luke 22:42
3. Col. 1:18–20 MSG

Chapter 13: You Are Allowed to Change

1. Kristen Strong, *Girl Meets Change* (Grand Rapids, MI: Revell, 2015), 76.
2. Gen. 12:1 GNT
3. Gen. 12:4
4. Matt. 1:1 CEV

Chapter 14: The Thing We're Most Afraid Of

1. Mark 4:29 MSG
2. Joel 1:11 BSB
3. Jennifer Dukes Lee, *It's All Under Control* (Carol Stream, IL: Tyndale House, 2018), 63.
4. Eccl. 3:3 ESV, emphasis added.
5. 1 Peter 2:24
6. Oswald Chambers, *My Utmost for His Highest* (Grand Rapids, MI: Discovery House, 2011), accessed on Kindle, 424.
7. James 1:2–4 NLT

8. Ann Voskamp, *The Broken Way* (Grand Rapids, MI: Zondervan, 2016), 21.
9. Gal. 6:9

Chapter 15: The Bleacher People

1. Amy Carmichael, *If* (Fort Washington, PA: CLC Publications, 2011), 43.
2. Mark 3:21
3. Mark 6:3
4. 1 Peter 2:23
5. 1 Cor. 4:3 NLT
6. Matt. 25:23

Chapter 16: How to Grow in the Dark

1. Kate Palmer, "Fall Is Favorite Season for Most Americans; 33% in Heartland Least Happy with the Weather," YouGov, June 10, 2013, https://today.yougov.com/topics/lifestyle/articles-reports /2013/06/10/fall-favorite-season-most-americans-33-heartland-l.

Chapter 17: The Slow, Healing Work of God

1. Eccl. 3:1, 5, emphasis added.
2. "Time Off & Vacation Usage," U.S. Travel Association, https:// www.ustravel.org/toolkit/time-and-vacation-usage.
3. "The Out-of-Office Blue," Alison Green, *Slate*, August 4, 2019, https://slate.com/human-interest/2019/08/vacation-stress -difficult-taking-time-off-work.html.
4. Eccl. 4:6 ESV
5. See Exodus 23:11.
6. Qtd. in *Hearts on Fire*, Michael Harter, ed., (Chicago: Loyola Press, 2005), 102–103. Reprinted with permission.

Chapter 18: The Five Things We Can't Afford to Forget

1. Prov. 16:9 NLT
2. Matt. 22:39

3. Eccl. 3:1 ESV
4. Eccl. 3:2 ESV
5. Eccl. 3:4 ESV
6. Eccl. 3:5 ESV
7. 2 Peter 1:3, emphasis added.

Chapter 19: A Time to Dance
1. Richard J. Foster, *Celebration of Discipline* (New York, NY: HarperCollins, 1978), 196.
2. Richard J. Foster, *Celebration of Discipline* (New York, NY: HarperCollins, 1978), 191.
3. John 15:11
4. Kim Ode, "Feeling Frantic? Disconnected? Isolated? Take a Moment to Learn about the Slow Movement." *Star Tribune*, January 7, 2017.

Chapter 20: Heaven Looks like a Farm
1. John 12:24–25 MSG
2. Rev. 22:1–3

Dig into Scripture to Slow Down and Grow Deep

We want to believe that a slower life is possible, but we are afraid of what we will miss if we don't keep up the pace. In this 6-week Bible study, Jennifer Dukes Lee weaves biblical lessons into her own experience of the importance of land, gleaned from her fifth-generation farm. The land—both then and now—teaches us how to un-hurry our hurry-sick hearts.

Growing Slow Bible Study
978-0-764-23836-9

From the Publisher

GREAT BOOKS

ARE EVEN BETTER WHEN THEY'RE SHARED!

Help other readers find this one:

- Post a review at your favorite online bookseller

- Post a picture on a social media account and share why you enjoyed it

- Send a note to a friend who would also love it—or better yet, give them a copy

Thanks for reading!

Printed in the USA
CPSIA information can be obtained
at www.ICGtesting.com
JSHW031709210624
65117JS00016B/483